ARGUING WELL

Argument is the primary way of discovering the truth and thinking freely for ourselves. But just knowing how to reason well is not enough to ensure that we do so because often factors seduce us away from reasoning well or at all. *Arguing Well* is a lucid introduction to the nature of good reasoning, how to test and construct good arguments. It assumes no prior knowledge of logic or philosophy. The book includes an accessible introduction to basic symbolic logic.

The book is ideal for any student embarking on academic study where arguments are what matter, in fact for all people who want to understand the nature and importance of good reasoning and awaken their ability to argue well.

John Shand is an Associate Lecturer in Philosophy at The Open University. He is the author of *Philosophy and Philosophers: An Introduction to Western Philosophy* (1994).

ARGUING WELL

John Shand

London and New York

TO JUDI WITH LOVE

First published 2000
by Routledge
11 New Fetter Lane, London EC4P 4EE

Simultaneously published in the USA and Canada
by Routledge
29 West 35th Street, New York, NY 10001

Routledge is an imprint of the Taylor & Francis Group

Transferred to Digital Printing 2003

© 2000 John Shand

Typeset in Sabon by Keystroke, Jacaranda Lodge, Wolverhampton

British Library Cataloguing in Publication Data
A catalogue record for this book is available from the British Library

Library of Congress Cataloging in Publication Data
Shand, John, 1956–
Arguing well / John Shand.
p. cm.
Includes bibliographical references.
1. Reasoning. I. Title.

BC177 .S45 2000
168—dc21   00–020475

ISBN 0–415–16685–3 (hbk)
ISBN 0–415–16686–1 (pbk)

Logic of itself cannot give anyone the answer to any question of substance; but without logic we often do not know the import of what we know and often fall into fallacy and inconsistency.

Peter Geach

Learning to infer is not just a matter of being taught about explicit logical relations between propositions; it is learning *to do* something.

Peter Winch

Thus Reason works itself out of the chains of dogma, of caprice, of arrogance, of passion. . . . It knows it is lost if it clutches prematurely at a part of the truth and makes it the ultimate absolute truth . . . it must not leave out anything, must not drop anything, exclude anything. It is itself a boundless openness. . . . Reason is like an open secret that can become known to anyone at any time; it is the quiet space into which everyone can enter through his own thought.

Karl Jaspers

To be clear-headed rather than confused; lucid rather than obscure; rational rather than otherwise; and to be neither more, nor less, sure of things than is justifiable by argument or evidence. That is worth trying for.

Geoffrey Warnock

CONTENTS

PREFACE

This book grew from a wish to give people the tools, both logical and psychological, that would enhance their reasoning and prevent them from abandoning reason, or applying it poorly, when applying it and applying it well is what they should be doing. Too many terrible consequences have followed throughout human history for this not to be important. Even regardless of that, reasoning is necessary for us to take control so that the kind of life we have is our genuine choice. This is only the beginning of course; the hard work comes in applying some of the precepts in this book. But without them, however you end up, you will be a sort of slave, not a freethinker. Anything else belittles us as human beings. There is no guarantee that such thinking will make you happier, but it can strengthen your integrity, and enhance a noble feature of human beings. It also builds on the unique capacity of human beings to reflect on themselves and the world. Here, integrity means trying to make one's beliefs hang together consistently and being determined to search for and face the truth even when we may wish the truth otherwise. Open argument is vital to this.

I am of course in the debt of several people who helped me with writing this book. In particular I should like to thank my wife Judith Shand, Sue Ashford, Michael Clark and Jay Kennedy; also the anonymous readers appointed by Routledge who commented on the manuscript. All remaining errors are strictly my responsibility.

INTRODUCTION

It matters how and when we argue. It matters because arguing is an indispensable way of getting to the truth and avoiding the false. If we do not use argument well and when we should, the likelihood is that we will acquire large numbers of false and quite probably dangerous beliefs on which we then base our actions. The calamitous consequences of the frequent death of reason in human history surely bears this out. Too many monolithic total-belief-systems have resulted in the closing down of rational thought for too many throughout history, engendering confusion and intolerance, for us to be complacent about this. This book aims to counter the seduction and weakness of abandoning, when we should not, rational argument. Sometimes we should not be reasoning; but even then there is usually a good rational argument why we should not be reasoning. More often we fail either to reason at all or to reason well when we should. To attain the habit of reasoning is one of the most important duties we have to ourselves. Go forth and argue.

This book is not intended as a textbook of logic or as a text for a course at all. Rather it hopes to serve as preparation for thinking, particularly for those newly engaged in academic work who have done little of such work in the recent past or indeed have done none at all. It is a guide, and in places a warning of the pitfalls, for anyone who would like to gain more confidence when dealing with rational argument.

It also advocates the view that what stands in the way of the proper application of reason has as much to do with seductive psychological forces that prevent us from reasoning when we

1

should as with an inability to understand the nature of good reasoning. Advice is given as to how these forces should be understood and dealt with. This is a matter of the greatest importance in our lives. If we are prone to being swayed into beliefs by forces beyond reason, which we then may act upon, forces that lead us to fail to apply reason when we should, and feel there is nothing wrong in this, then all sorts of harmful and destructive beliefs will follow. The book modestly hopes to do something to alert the reader to this greatly underrated danger. My hope is that the book will make the reader active when engaged with arguments, either in being on the receiving end or delivering them. It is, in other words, a guide to what you should be doing when assessing or constructing arguments and to the ways of avoiding the dangers that often, by stealth and seduction, blunt or crush our reason, prevent it from even getting off the ground, when it should be paramount, and truth our goal.

The book outlines clearly what is involved in being engaged in the assessment and construction of arguments (Chapters 2–5), and what steps one can take to make sure one is thus engaged (Chapters 1 and 6).

1

RATIONALE

1.1 The overall purpose of this book is to present the basic tools and principles of good reasoning in arguments, and to suggest how one might acquire habitual mechanisms to overcome causal forces that would undermine reasoning. It is meant as a precursor to, and preparation for, any course that involves the assessment and construction of arguments. But it is also hoped that the book contains ideas that the reader will find interesting in themselves and be able to apply generally in the conduct of his life.

1.2 It is made clear in the book what the value of reasoning is, and that the nature of reason *as such* is logically distinct from the psychological processes involved in acquiring beliefs. *Using* reason, that is the act of *reasoning*, is a psychological process, and is also distinct from reason as such. Reasoning is one way of acquiring beliefs, indeed a way that has merits that are here defended, but good reasoning is not defined by its being a route to belief. A process of reasoning may or may not lead to a belief at the end of it. Reasoning is not, insofar as it is good or bad, concerned with the outcome of someone's having a belief, but with whether that belief is justified. A sharp distinction is made here between logic and rhetoric (in the broad sense): between processes leading to our coming to conclusions (rhetoric) and our being justified in holding those conclusions on the basis of argument (logic). Reasoning may as a matter of fact convince us of a proposition, but we can be presented with a piece of reasoning that is perfectly sound whether this is the outcome or not.

The aim of the book is twofold:

(a) It will enable the reader to assess writings or assess speech more *actively*, when the purpose of that assessment is the quality of arguments; and it will enable the reader to *construct* better arguments more consciously when writing and speaking, when it is the quality of arguments that is the primary concern.

(b) It will enable the reader to better counter those forces that would tend to cause the reader to reason badly or not at all in circumstances where they should be reasoning.

1.3 There are theoretical arguments behind the book, which are partly contentious, but a consideration of these will I hope deepen readers' appreciation of the notion of reason and reasoning. The theoretical contention of the author is that the notion of good reasoning can be reduced to a certain basic idea. That idea is *deductive soundness* as defined by the notions of *validity* and *truth*. This makes the distinction between good and bad reasoning decisively, because if anything counts as good reasoning then deductive reasoning does. The aim here is not so much to make this theoretical point as to give readers a useful tool with which to assess the merits of arguments that they encounter in their reading or in speech, and with which to construct arguments of their own.

The view here is essentially a reductionist one with regard to good reasoning and fallacies. Good reasoning can be reduced to a single notion, that of deductive soundness: (a) the premises must be *true* and (b) the argument *valid* so that the conclusion follows from the premises, in that to assert the premises and deny the conclusion would involve a *contradiction*, that is, would be inconsistent. It is from (a) and (b) alone that an argument giving one a reason to accept a conclusion as true is ultimately derived. Included in the analysis of validity is that it is a matter of *form*, and that one should not be distracted by irrelevant content in assessing validity. Individual arguments are valid because they are instances of valid forms of argument: valid *argument-forms*. In this way, it is hoped, the notion of good reasoning can be applied to any situation irrespective of subject matter.

1.4 What are often referred to as 'fallacies' are not significant because they are errors in formal reasoning – such errors are usually so obvious as to be hardly worth pointing out – but rather because they are psychological rhetorical tricks designed to fool people into thinking they have been presented with a good argument when they have not, in order to convince them of a conclusion. This may be because there is no good argument for the conclusion. To avoid fallacies it is only required that one stick by the principles of good reasoning – the conclusion really follows from the true premises – in this way all fallacies collapse together. The distinctive feature of what are often called fallacies is not their formal failure to abide by the rules of deductive soundness – although they may do this too – but rather their effectiveness as psychological tricks whereby someone thinks they have been presented with a good argument when they have not. The only true fallacy in the end is the one where there has been a failure to argue with deductive soundness: true premises and a valid argument.

1.5 In addition it is a theoretical contention of this book that the *only* thing that can give one a good reason for a belief or an action is that there is a sound argument for it, one whereby the conclusion is the belief in question or the conclusion is a prescription that the action in question should occur. Neither beliefs nor facts about the world can in themselves give one a reason to believe or do anything. Either may *cause* one to have other beliefs or act, but that is distinct from having a reason. That this is not obvious is obscured by the banality of latent and tacit arguments that give the false impression that we move directly from belief or fact to a conclusion. However, if one has a reason at all to believe or act, there must be a good argument – an argument that will most likely connect other beliefs or facts to the final belief or act in a structure of normative justification. Facts and beliefs, as with causal processes, are in themselves logically inert; they have no bearing alone as to whether one has reasons. Only when linked in an *argument* do they have rational force.

For example, it might be said that I have a reason not to climb down a cliff if I believe it to be crumbly or I have a reason because it is in fact crumbly – but neither belief nor fact of itself gives me a reason. It only seems to because we tacitly presuppose a good argument (or at least an argument), something along the following rough lines perhaps.

I do not want to hurt myself and die
Crumbly rocks on cliffs like these if climbed down are a
   likely way to hurt oneself or die
These rocks are crumbly or I believe them to be so

———————————

Therefore, I should not climb down the cliff

This contention applies even to cases where simple perception is involved. One might think that I have a reason for believing there is a glass of water in front of me if I can see it. But built into 'see' here is an argument, familiar to philosophers if not to others, linking my having the experience of seeing a glass of water with my having a reason for believing that there is a glass of water. Indeed it is a matter of philosophical debate just how strong this argument can be – but however that turns out, an argument is essential for my being justified, my having a reason. In short there is an argument that seeing the glass in given circumstances is a good reason for believing there is a glass to be seen. My merely seeing the glass of itself implies nothing. It is in fact not hard to think of cases where we might be deluded. Again, whatever one thinks of that, one is always involved in an argument, and one is tacitly saying there is a good argument when contending that a certain belief is true or one has a reason to act in a certain way. It is just that most of the time, through familiarity, we do not notice that such latent arguments are tacitly assumed.

1.6 An important distinction is made between the *objective* failure (and success) of arguments and the *person-directed* failure (and success) of arguments. A successful argument gives a reason for its conclusion being true. In the *objective* sense an argument is a success if it is an instance of a valid argument-form, where contradiction would be involved in asserting the premises and denying the conclusion, and if it involves only true premises. If someone is presented with such an argument, he has been given a good reason for accepting the conclusion as true in the objective sense whether he (or anyone else) does so or not. However, even if someone is presented with such an argument it may not give *him* a good reason for accepting the conclusion as true. Thus an argument may fail in the person-directed sense because the person to whom it is directed may be unable to accept the premises as true or see that it is valid. The argument may be successful in the objective sense – *have* true premises and *be* valid – yet fail in the person-directed sense because a person cannot accept the premises or that it is valid. Note the obverse is not the case: an argument cannot be a success in the person-directed sense and yet fail in the objective sense. If an argument fails in the objective sense – either because it contains false premises or is invalid, or both – it cannot give anyone a good reason for the truth of the conclusion, that is a reason in the person-directed sense, because it does not give a reason at all, whatever people viewing the argument may think about it and however acceptable they may find it. A person may think an argument gives him a reason to accept a conclusion as true, but if it is not a good argument in the objective sense then he is mistaken.

It should be noted that the objective and person-directed distinction is not a matter of psychology but a purely conceptual one. In the person-directed sense arguments fail, not because they fail to convince as a matter of psychological fact, but because, in the sense of a person either not knowing whether the premises are true, or being unable to see that the conclusion follows from the premises, *that person* has not been given a reason to believe the conclusion is true – although in the objective sense he may have been given such a reason. In such cases, for an argument to be a person-directed success I may need elucidation and perhaps further justification given to the premises – the premises that I find unacceptable will form the conclusion of another argument that I can accept – and in that way I can accept the conclusion of the original argument. It is not a matter of convincing me but of giving *me* a justification. All that is needed for the objective success of an argument is that its premises be true and it be valid, in which case the conclusion is true, whether anyone can see these things or not. Indeed it might be the case that no one can know if an argument has premises that are true (we might have no access to information that would confirm the premises), or if the argument is valid (it might be so complex as to be beyond our comprehension), for practical reasons or even in principle, but for all that it could be a good argument in the objective sense.

1.7 Let me give an example of how the objective and person-directed distinction works in practice. It is, in the person-directed sense, as far as being presented with a good argument is concerned, no use for an oncologist to present to me an argument that I have cancer on the basis of premises that are unacceptable to me either because I do not know if they are true or because they are beyond my understanding. Similarly, it is, in the person-directed sense, as far as being presented with a good argument is concerned, no use for an oncologist to present to me an argument that I have cancer whose validity I cannot see, perhaps because it is beyond my comprehension. If I am to be given a good reason for accepting the conclusion as true on the basis *of an argument* (as opposed to accepting the conclusion by trusting that the oncologist *has* a good argument and knows his job), then I must be given an argument that I can see to be valid and that has premises that I can accept, even if the original argument was perfectly good in the objective sense in both being valid and having true premises. I must be given a good argument in the person-directed sense. If my doctor tells me I have cancer, and I do not understand the argument or know whether the premises are true, so I cannot see rationally how he comes to his conclusion, then to give *me* a good argument the doctor needs to argue in some simpler way that I do understand and can accept. Obviously there are limits to how simple and basic arguments can get.

Of course I might just accept the oncologist's conclusion anyway; but one should do this not on trust (whatever that means) or because he is a 'specialist' as such, but because we think he is arguing validly from true premises whether I can see it or not. If he has such an argument, then the conclusion that I have cancer is true. Of course the conclusion may be true anyway, but if it does not follow from true premises validly, then there is no argument for its being true. The appeal to the authority of a cancer specialist as to whether I have cancer might look in a sense like a good argument in itself – but this is an illusion except insofar as by 'cancer specialist' we mean someone much more able than most to marshal good arguments in the objective sense in the field of cancer. The real question is not what a person is called, or what authority he is supposed to have, but whether he is good at constructing good arguments: validly deducing conclusions from true premises.

1.8 It is sometimes argued that deductive reasoning alone is too restrictive to characterise what is permissible as good reasoning: that there are other non-deductive modes of reasoning that are perfectly legitimate, depending on the circumstances. This includes supposed arguments that are based on, for example, authority, emotion, popular opinion and of course induction, that are said to be legitimate in certain circumstances. This I believe is a mistake. In each case the putatively legitimate modes of non-deductive reasoning are only so because they are tacitly dependent on the basic notion of deduction. The confusion arises because this is not seen, but instead the legitimacy of the argument is ascribed to the surface circumstances and the fact that one may come up with true beliefs. But coming up with true beliefs is not enough to show that the method by which one does so constitutes a good *argument*, or indeed an argument at all – for this there needs to be given a *reason* for the belief even if it is true, and for that it must come as the conclusion of a piece of sound deduction. In all cases either there is an argument where by starting from true premises and moving with deductive validity one could derive the conclusion, or there is not – and if there is not, despite the appearance, such as appealing to an authority, one does not have a reason for accepting the conclusion as true.

There is a belief that there must be legitimate forms of reasoning weaker than deduction if we are to do justice to our actual reasoning. But this confuses the nature of good reasoning – which is deductive – with our ability to know the truth of the premises required to turn these weaker forms into pieces of sound deduction. Often we have to be satisfied with reasoning that is less than deductively perfect not because the less perfect reasoning is legitimate in itself, but because we are unable to know the truth of premises that would turn it into a deductive piece of reasoning. So we leave them out. But if it is justifiable for us to believe the conclusion true at all *on the basis of an argument*, such premises have to be true and the argument valid.

1.9 One common source of legitimate reasoning other than deduction is said to be *induction*. Inductive arguments are such that their conclusions go beyond the content of their premises. One might argue from the premise that 'All observed swans are white' to the conclusion that 'All swans are white'. Deductively this is fallacious in that the premises could be true and the conclusion could be false without any contradiction being involved

– in fact the conclusion is false. To see induction itself as a legitimate form of reasoning is I believe an error. It is legitimate only insofar as it is seen as a form of deductive reasoning with suppressed premises. Indeed, all non-deductive reasoning should be looked upon as *enthymemes*: that is, deductive arguments, if they are arguments at all, with missing premises. The question of whether premises can be established as true is an entirely separate matter from what constitutes good reasoning. If we cannot establish premises as true in order to turn an argument into a deductively sound one, then so much the worse for that argument; it should not lead us to concoct spurious legitimation for the supposed 'validity' of forms of reasoning, such as induction, which are weaker than sound deduction. The premises required to turn the weaker forms into sound deduction may just *be* true, in which case their inclusion gives a reason for the conclusion being true whether we can know those premises are true or not. Our inability to establish them as true should not lead us to proffer anything other than deductive soundness as reasoning proper.

What might turn an inductive argument into a deductive one would be the addition, in any case of inductive reasoning, of a Uniformity of Nature Principle. Indeed, without such a premise it is difficult to see how anything very much follows from the premises usually found in inductive reasoning. The Uniformity of Nature Principle will say something like: there are laws of nature, and they hold universally in both space and time. Take the following inductive argument:

All observed free rocks near the surface of the earth fall towards the centre of the earth

Therefore, this free rock near the surface of the earth will fall towards the centre of the earth

This is an incredibly feeble, and plainly invalid, piece of reasoning unless some Uniformity of Nature Principle is included in the argument, along with a universal natural law about the behaviour of rocks and gravity. It is a notoriously difficult problem in philosophy to justify the Uniformity of Nature Principle: its denial does not imply a contradiction, and yet the attempt to establish it by observation is bound to be circular. But the difficulty, perhaps impossibility, of establishing the Uniformity of Nature Principle as true should neither lead us to think of inductive reasoning as a legitimate form of reasoning, nor lead us to think its inclusion, which would make the inductive reasoning deductive, irrational. The same applies to the problem of establishing the required universal natural laws. The Uniformity of Nature Principle for all we know might just *be* true. If it is, then its inclusion in pieces of inductive reasoning to make them deductive means we have a perfectly good reason for accepting the conclusion of such reasoning as true. Again, we should not take our inability to know the truth of premises to imply that we do not *have*, if the argument is valid, a sound deductive argument for the conclusion being true in the objective sense: if the premises *are* true, and the argument *is* valid, the conclusion *is* true.

1.10 Another argument for supposing that there are weaker forms of reasoning than deduction is the mistaken belief that if only deductive reasoning were valid in our reasoning about the world, that would somehow bind the world to a course of deductive necessity described in a set of necessary truths, when it is in fact contingent (could have been otherwise). But this fear arises from confusion regarding the move from the premises to the conclusion being necessary in deduction – because the negation of the conclusion would form a contradiction with those premises – with the premises being necessary. It is perfectly proper for the premises of a deductive argument to be contingent, and if so the conclusion will be contingent too. Deduction shows, if the premises are true, what other truths must follow as conclusions. But that does not mean the conclusions are necessary truths (could not be otherwise).

By self-contradiction is meant a proposition of the form (p & $\sim p$); for example, 'It is raining and it is not raining'. A self-contradictory proposition both asserts and denies the same fact; it says it is both true and false that something is the case; it asserts something and at the same time asserts its opposite. If the negation of a proposition is a self-contradiction it is a necessary truth. If the assertion of a proposition is a self-contradiction it is a necessary falsehood. In all other cases – the negation is not self-contradictory and its assertion is not self-contradictory – a proposition is contingent: it could be true or it could be false.

11

To say that in a valid deductive argument if the premises are true the conclusion must be true is not to say that the conclusion must be true in that a denial of the conclusion would be *self-contradictory* – which would show it to be a necessary truth – but only to show that its denial would contradict the premises. Deduction shows what must be true *if* the premises are true. Unless the premises are necessary truths, deduction is perfectly compatible with conclusions being contingent.

> All men are mortal
> Socrates is a man
> ───────────────
> Socrates is mortal

This is a valid argument. There is nothing self-contradictory about negating the conclusion and asserting 'Socrates is not mortal', although it may be false. The argument only shows that if the premises are true, then the conclusion must follow and be true. But of course there is nothing self-contradictory about negating the premises and asserting 'All men are not mortal' and 'Socrates is not a man', although these assertions may be false. So if the premises are contingent, then so is the conclusion, even in a deductively valid argument. The conclusion has no more necessity than the premises. It would be a mistake to abandon deduction when reasoning about the empirical world because we think, rightly, that the truths about the world are not necessary ones. Only in mathematics and logic does one find such necessary truths. But to reason deductively about the empirical world does not presuppose that one thinks that truths about the world are necessary ones.

1.11 Where does this leave the commonsense notion of giving a good argument for something when that argument may be less than fully deductively sound? There is a perfectly normal sense, which follows common usage, in which something less than a deductively sound argument counts as a 'good argument'. Take the following case.

> I left my book that is now missing in my room an hour ago
> You are the only other person in the house
> ───────────────
> Conclusion: You have taken the book from my room

This looks like a 'good argument' in the ordinary sense: we would normally be quite happy to say that the conclusion follows from the premises. But does it? I suggest that the argument only appears to be a good argument because we tacitly turn it into a deductively valid argument. As it stands it is not deductively valid. This can be tested by asking whether it is possible for the premises to be true and the conclusion false. The answer is surely yes. To put it another way, we can ask if there would be a contradiction between the premises and the negation of the conclusion. The answer is surely no. The reason it is thought to be a good argument is that there are all sorts of missing premises, of a more or less daft and far-fetched nature, that we tacitly use to make the argument work, some of which are the result of arguments we already accept. The conclusion could be false, even if the premises are true, if, for example, books could move around on their own, or aliens had materialised in my room and abducted the book, or I had gone mad and could not remember anything for more than ten minutes. All of these conjectures are outlandish of course, but not logically impossible, and in the right circumstances not even that improbable. That we happen not to take them seriously is often a result of conclusions we have drawn from reasoning elsewhere.

1.12 Another example. Someone shouts 'Fire!' with great conviction as an 'argument' for why we should get out of the building – the conclusion 'I should get out of the building' does not of course follow logically – but in this case I would be foolish to stop to ask for a proper argument along the lines of 'The building is on fire, if you stay you will die a horrible death, you do not want to die a horrible death, therefore you should get out of the building', nor would it be sensible for the person who shouted 'Fire!' to think of presenting one. However, the reason that merely hearing 'Fire!' appears to be a good reason for drawing the conclusion that leads to one's acting here is that some such sound argument is assumed to lie behind a sincere shout of 'Fire!'. There is indeed a good *argument* for saying that this is not an appropriate situation for presenting traditional good arguments, but rather we should just shout 'Fire!'. But this does not mean we have found a new argument-form in which merely shouting 'Fire!' is a good argument.

1.13 Readers of books of critical reasoning are often told, in assessing the validity of non-deductive arguments, to think of ways in which the conclusion could be false even though the premises are true. But, unless the argument in question is deductive, this gives the reader no guide at all as to what is a valid argument because it gives him no guide as to what is to count as a reasonable speculation in which the conclusion is supposed false while the premises are still true. In all but the case of a deductively sound argument there are numerous ways, perhaps infinite in number, in which the conclusion could be false although the premises are true. The only way of assessing the truth or falsity of the speculations we may posit is to draw them as conclusions of other arguments. And these arguments had better be deductive in form, unlike the original one, or we embark on an infinite regress of arguments with no method of assessing their validity or that of any argument.

1.14 All this points to my contention that the core idea of a good argument is deductive soundness, and that arguments are better the closer they get to being deductively sound. One starts with true premises and what would, if denied, form a contradiction with those premises is true. In this deductive sense the conclusion *follows* from the premises: if *these* premises are true, then deductively *this* follows. I know of no other way in which conclusions truly *follow* from premises.

1.15 It will perhaps be argued that in life people will not find real arguments set out in a strictly deductive way, clearly recognisable as cases of deductive reasoning. This is of course true. But that is no reason for concluding that there are forms of reasoning weaker than sound deduction that are legitimate arguments in their own right. They are legitimate because they can be made into deductive arguments with premises that are true (*objective* success) and perhaps also with premises we can accept as true (*person-directed* success). This is overlooked because often what would prevent an argument being deductively sound can be dismissed as silly, and what is required can be accepted as obvious – in such cases, without going through the process of doing this, we are in the normal sense justified in accepting the conclusions as true, and do so on the basis of a good argument. 'Real arguments' do not exhibit a new and legitimate type of reasoning over and above the more formal examples; they do not have a different logic all of their own, as opposed to the artificially constructed examples. Rather they are, insofar as they are any good as arguments, arguments that must obey the same rules as any argument, but they are written with various degrees of complexity and obscurity. Complex and obscure arguments, if they are any good, are made up of simple parts that are sound.

It is not helpful, in thinking about the arguments we may encounter in life, to present people with a list of forbidden and permitted rules, apart from those that characterise deductive soundness. Deduction is the clear basic notion that permits of no exceptions. The attempt to codify rules for the complexities of 'real arguments' would give us a distracting array of dos and don'ts that it would be impossible to apply. Nor does the attempt to codify such rules do justice to the fine-grained flexibility of our intelligence – indeed it is this very flexibility that is surely the defining feature of the superiority of human intelligence. To criticise the approach here is rather like criticising a book on good driving for not giving rules to deal with all possible road situations: not only would such a rulebook be impossible, but the attempt to use it would produce something at best useless, and at worst dangerous. We all know that beyond the novice level the best way to get good at something is simply to do it; it is in that way that we ultimately learn and improve.

1.16 What I present here is the basic notion of good reasoning: what good reasoning is if anything counts as good reasoning. The only way to get better at reasoning, beyond this basic guide as to what is essential, is to *do* it. This is not only in order to get skilled at reasoning, but also to get into the habit of reasoning so that we fight off forces that cause us to abandon reason when we should not. As people look at arguments they should ask themselves:

(a) Are the premises true?
(b) Is the argument valid?

If the answer to one or both questions is 'no', then the argument has failed in the sense of not giving a reason for the truth of the conclusion. The conclusion may be true, but a reason has not been given for its being true. The examiner of the argument can then go on to introduce refinements to particular cases, refinements that are too complex to be characterisable or useful as rules.

1.17 I do not discuss the nature of *truth* in the book. This is because it is an epistemological matter that is outside the scope of this book. I merely assume, sufficient to my purpose, that there is some sense in which propositions can be said to be true or false, and that all propositions are either true or false. That this is so of propositions is sufficient to characterise the nature of good reasoning. But it can be said that propositions, which may be premises in arguments, can *be* true (or false) independently of whether anyone can know them to be so or not. This is the distinction between something being true and my thinking it so. There is an unproblematic sense in which people would agree that there is such a notion of truth. For example, it is true that spiders generally either get into baths by crawling up the plug hole or by falling in after crawling around the edge and then being unable to climb up the smooth sides. The former is a common belief, but in fact the latter is true. The notion of good reasoning does not depend on any particular notion of truth, merely that there is one.

How, or indeed if, the premises of an argument are established as true is not a matter for reasoning as such, in that we do not have to be committed to how, or if, this may happen in order to characterise good reasoning. All that is required to characterise good reasoning is that the premises be true and the stated conclusion is such that its denial would contradict those premises.

1.18 Reiterating the point made in §1.5, I contend that in a sense arguments are the only way to establish the truth of propositions, including premises – which may form the content of our beliefs and the basis of our reasons to act. This is again strictly speaking a claim outside the scope of the book, but if true emphasises the importance of argument. So I shall say something more to defend the claim. It might be said that propositions are often shown to be true not by following from other true propositions, but by a comparison with experience – by looking at how things are in the world. Suppose we want to establish some truth such as the mundane 'The cat is on the mat'. Now suppose that we try to confirm the premise by looking towards the mat to see if the cat is on it. Suppose it appears to be. Does this experience of itself support the claim that the proposition 'The cat is on the mat' is true? If we think so it is only because we unwittingly accept various implied arguments. For the having of the experience to imply that the statement 'The cat is on the mat' is true there has to be some kind of argument involved. It may be as straight-forward as: from *that* kind of experience in these circumstances we can safely conclude that the proposition 'The cat is on the mat' is true. Whatever the argument, there is some kind of argument involved that connects the experience to the legitimacy of holding certain things as true on the basis of it. Many philosophers have claimed that even establishing the most basic truths about the world on the basis of experience is problematic. The mere directing of someone to experience without an argument involved would show nothing. On the basis of the same experience of seeing a cat, if we knew we were under the influence of a hallucinogenic drug, we might well rightly conclude, remembering that we do not own a cat, that there is *not* a cat on the mat, or that the cat is a football. In any case there must be some argument about how our knowledge depends on our experience in general, and in each case that experience in particular, for propositions to be implied as conclusions of our experiences.

In general, apart from truths that can be known because their denial is self-contradictory such as 2+2=4 (its denial being 1+1+1+1 ≠ 1+1+1+1), truths are known by how they stand in relation to the world we experience, such as 'London has more than 5 million people living in it'.

1.19 Much emphasis is also given in this book to factors beyond reason, that lead to the undermining or even total abandonment of reasoning. The things that lead people to reason badly, or not at all, are often not a lack of understanding of good reasoning – the need to go from true premises to conclusions that follow from those premises – but rather a sort of psychological blindness induced by factors outside the reasoning process. These forces can be countered through acquiring good mental habits that form an opposing force, causing one to reason when one should. Such habits can be acquired best and strengthened through practising reasoning especially about those matters we find it hard to reason about – not so much because the reasoning involved is complex and hard work (although we may give up when we ought not to because of that) – but because we find it is psychologically uncomfortable to apply reason to these matters. They may be cherished beliefs; ones whose loss we think might bring fear and sadness; ones that we have simply accepted for a long time; ones that concern emotive issues it is hard to be cool-headed about; ones that we feel we must believe because they are thought true by someone whom we love or respect; ones embedded in a long cultural tradition; ones that we feel under pressure from those around us to believe – ones that we may believe for a host of causes that make it hard for us to apply reason to them. In this way, if we can apply reason in these difficult cases, we will be stronger in being more likely to apply reason in any other case when we should be doing so.

This is not to conflate logic and psychology, but on the contrary to emphasise the distinction between *arguments* and *power*; between what constitutes a good reasoning process justifying a conclusion and the causal process leading to a belief; what *is* a good argument and what may *produce* belief. These two matters are logically independent. Of course when someone reasons there is a causal process going on in their head; but whether it is good reasoning or not is completely independent of the course or outcome of that causal process. What defines good reasoning is prescriptive or normative, not descriptive. The goodness of the reasoning is defined by truth and validity – the nature of reason – not what happens causally as a matter of fact. The inclination to reason and the act of reasoning, but not reason itself, is a causal process and it therefore has some power to bring us to hold certain beliefs. But we cannot be confident that the natural innate inclination is strong enough to induce us to start or once started to continue because there are non-rational forces ranged against it. This is not to contradict what has just been said about the strict independence of reason as such from causes, for what we are talking about here is not anything that characterises the nature of reason itself, but only what happens when someone does some reasoning. So often the act of reasoning is weak and easily deflected, or not started at all, in just those cases when it should be. Because of this I have dwelt upon the importance of building up causal counter-forces whereby we reason when we should and reason well. These forces that undermine our reasoning well – our arguing well – are neglected in discussions of good reasoning, as if once the rules are laid out the job is done. But that is only the beginning. Practising reasoning, doing it, especially in hard cases, is what helps. It is no use whatsoever knowing what good reasoning is if one fails to reason when one should. Finding the way to reason when one should is too important to be neglected. It is in fact perhaps the most important thing any human being can do.

2

ARGUMENTS

2.1 An *argument* is a set of *propositions* where one of the set (the *conclusion*) is supposed to *follow from* the others (the *premises*). If it is the case that the premises are true, and the conclusion does indeed follow from the premises, then the argument provides evidence or rational grounds or a reason that the conclusion is true.

2.2 *Propositions* are any grammatical form that can be either true or false. Another way of putting this is to say that propositions are the meaning of the sentences which say something true or false. Different sentences in the same or indeed different languages can express the same proposition. An example of this is the following.

Jack loves Jean.
Jean is loved by Jack.

Although these are different sentences, they say the same thing, and that thing can be either true or false. Logic has no interest in the different ways in which the same meanings can be expressed; it is concerned only with the sameness of meaning.

'The cat is on the mat' expresses a proposition. For the sake of brevity in this book I shall call such linguistic forms propositions and drop talk of sentences. Propositions may be either true or false, but not both. Other grammatical forms cannot be either true or false at all. Questions such as 'Why did the chicken cross the road?', and commands such as 'Shut the window', cannot be either true or false. Given this understanding of propositions, it can be said that arguments consist of collections of propositions that are related to one another in a particular way. An argument is not just a pile of propositions. A telephone book lists names according to the structure dictated by having them arranged alphabetically. An argument is a collection of propositions with a particular *argumentative* structure. If a collection of propositions constitutes an argument there are specific putative relations between the propositions that make it an argument.

2.3 The relations that make collections of propositions into an argument can be characterised as follows. The *premise* or *premises* of an argument are those propositions in the argument from which the conclusion is said to follow. The *conclusion* is that proposition which is said to follow from the premise or premises.

Argument = [premise/s (propositions) ⇒ conclusion (proposition)]

As it is set out in a piece of writing the conclusion does not always appear after the premises. A writer or speaker may present a conclusion and then give the premises from which he thinks it follows. But this makes no difference to what it is for something to be an argument.

2.4 It should be noted that the terms 'premise' and 'conclusion' are relative terms. Leaving philosophical niceties aside it can be said that no proposition is absolutely a premise or absolutely a conclusion. A conclusion of a particular argument may get used as a premise in a further argument. Indeed such chains of arguments are very common. The premise of a particular argument may become the conclusion of a further argument when, for example, the premise requires justification.

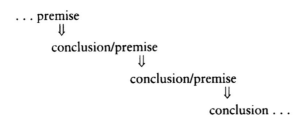

The diagram can be read two ways. We can read it downwards, in which case we are viewing a chain of reasoning where conclusions of previous arguments get used as premises in new arguments to produce further conclusions. We can read it upwards, in which case premises become the conclusions of previous arguments that follow from other premises.

It might seem that arguments are often more complex than this and that the structure outlined above does not do justice to this fact. For example two different premises might be presented as leading to the same conclusion. But in this case what one really has is two arguments. One just has to separate them out. So the basic structure of argumentation is fundamentally as just given above.

2.5 The value of arguments is that they are a way of finding out what it is rational to believe or think true. We know that if an argument is a good argument, the premises are true and the conclusion follows from the premises, then we are rationally justified in believing the conclusion of that argument or accepting it as true.

2.6 One way of characterising *logic* is to say that it is the study of good and bad *forms* of argument. Logic hopes to isolate all those forms of arguments that can be said to be good ones. In this sense logic is not concerned with the truth of particular propositions or indeed with the contents of particular arguments. Rather it is concerned with isolating those forms of argument where *if* the premises are true there is a rational justification for holding that the conclusion is true. That is, logic hopes to identify the general form of those collections of propositions where the conclusion really does follow from the premises. Once one knows the *forms* of good argument, one can confidently slot particular propositions into those forms, and be sure that the outcome is a good argument in that particular case. This is because any propositions slotted into a good argument *form* will be a good *argument*.

2.7 Logic is concerned with the *form* of arguments, not particular arguments, similar to the way that a cookery-book is concerned with the form of a certain dish. Thus a recipe identifies the constituents of any good apple pie; it gives you a plan; it is not concerned with any particular apple pie made in a particular kitchen. Logic is like a very exact and precise set of recipes. Just as any cook who follows the recipe will, by exactly following the rules, produce a good particular apple pie, so anyone who presents an argument using one of the good forms of argument will produce a good particular argument.

2.8 Logic must be sharply distinguished from what might generally be called *rhetoric*. Rhetoric is the art of persuasion using language; its overriding concern is that of the power or efficacy with which it can, as a matter of psychological fact, bring about belief in a certain conclusion. In doing this, rhetoric is not committed to using good arguments. Contrary to first appearances, arguments – the form of which logic studies – are not essentially about persuading or getting someone to hold a certain belief or accept a certain proposition as true. There are many ways to get someone to hold certain beliefs or accept certain propositions that are not arguments: brainwashing, depriving someone of sleep and repeating something again and again; holding a gun to a person's head and demanding that he agrees; flattering a person in some way that induces him to believe you; or a fine orator may use some dramatic means that persuades the crowd to trust his word. What may as a matter of fact get someone to hold a certain belief or accept certain propositions as true is a purely psychological matter, and has no bearing on whether something is a good argument or not. Presenting someone with an argument is one way, it so happens sometimes a good way, to get someone to believe something or to hold a proposition as true. But this is not its prime aim or part of the essential nature of arguments. The prime aim of an argument is to present a rational justification for a belief or for the truth of a proposition, and this is totally independent of whether it in fact convinces anyone or not. To show that the issue of what is convincing and what is rationally justified are totally distinct, we only have to consider the following two true propositions:

1   There could in principle be a good argument that gives rational grounds for accepting the conclusion that as a matter of psychological fact convinces nobody: a good argument, but psychologically unpersuasive.

    Of course what is psychologically unpersuasive will depend on the nature of the individual to whom the argument is directed. But below are examples of arguments that are good arguments whose conclusions many people might find difficult to believe true.

Example: In a lottery where one selects any 6 numbers from 1–49, because each number is selected at random, the numbers 123456 (in some order) are just as likely to come up as any other combination of six numbers.

Example: A cannonball and a feather dropped in a vacuum from the same height will reach the ground at the same time, because when gravity pulls on things the strength of the pull and the resistance to the pull are both proportional to the mass, and so balance each other: thus the resultant acceleration is equal for all objects.

2   There could in principle be a poor argument that gives no rational grounds for accepting the conclusion that as a matter of psychological fact convinces everybody: psychologically persuasive, but a bad argument.

Which bad argument people find convincing will depend on the nature of the individual, but below are arguments that are bad but whose conclusions many might believe true on the basis of the argument given.

The cases where this happens are often far from trivial. Adolf Hitler in powerful oratory put forward the argument that because the Jews were like verminous rats, akin to a disease, they should therefore be exterminated; millions accepted this conclusion despite this being a bad argument. Hundreds, perhaps thousands, of women were tortured and killed in the Middle Ages because the Catholic Church contended they were witches possessed by the devil; many people accepted this conclusion and aided in the identification and burning of 'witches'. Joseph Stalin identified millions of people whom he argued were a threat to what was a marvellous revolution and these people should therefore be killed, tortured, starved or imprisoned in terrible conditions; many people accepted (some still do) this conclusion and actively or passively cooperated. And so it goes on today.

Below are some more prosaic examples of arguments that people might tend to find psychologically convincing even though they are in fact bad arguments.

Example: Since things even themselves out in the long run, after I have tossed a coin 1000 times and got all heads, the

1001st toss is more likely to be a tail than a head and its occurring is more than a 50/50 chance.

Example: A cannonball dropped from the top of the mast of a boat will, because the boat is moving forward while the cannonball is falling, fall not at the foot of the mast, but some way further behind the mast towards the stern of the boat.

The two propositions above in §2.8, taken together, show that the question of what is an argument that gives one rational grounds for holding a belief, and what in fact determines the beliefs people hold, are theoretically quite distinct. For this reason it is said that the rules of good reasoning are *prescriptive* or *normative*, not descriptive of what people might or might not do: they lay down standards or norms that say what we *ought* to do if we want to reason well, regardless of what we in fact do and even regardless of whether nobody or everybody does it. A good argument may in fact be a convincing argument too; but whether it is a good argument is quite independent of whether it is convincing or not. Thus, that a certain form of argument is a good argument is not dependent on a show of hands agreeing that it is or it is not a good argument; it is or it is not a good argument regardless of what people think. In the same way 2+2=4 is true regardless of whether everyone or no-one accepts it as true.

The distinction between logic and rhetoric is in fact a commonplace. We all know of times when we have been swayed into believing something, when in fact we have been given no good reason for believing that thing – think of the persuasive salesman who induces us to think his product is the best while in fact presenting no good argument for the conclusion. We all know of times when, although we have been presented with a good argument, we still refuse to believe the conclusion of that argument – think of the unpersuasive scientist who fails to induce us to abandon a cherished belief while in fact presenting a good argument for his conclusion.

Before going on to look at the matter in more detail, it is important to notice that the conclusion of a bad argument, or indeed of no argument at all, can still be true; but if it is true, and we have not been given a good argument for that conclusion, the point is that we have not been given a *reason* for believing it true.

If we hit upon the truth without actually using arguments, or by some path which can be ratified by its implying tacitly or immanently a good argument, we will have done so by accident, a sort of guess. It is one way of going on, but it is not a reliable way of discovering or deciding on the truth.

2.9 *Propositions* are true or they are false. *Arguments* are valid or they are invalid. It makes no sense to say that a proposition is valid or invalid, or that an argument is true or false.

2.10 An argument is *valid* if the conclusion *follows from* the premises. The conclusion follows from the premises if to assert the premises but deny the conclusion would be a *contradiction* or *inconsistent*. One commits a contradiction if one both asserts and denies the same proposition, or to put it another way, one commits a contradiction if one both asserts a proposition and asserts the opposite of that proposition, that is its *negation*. If one asserts together 'It is raining' and 'It is not raining', thus asserting that 'It is raining and it is not raining', one is asserting a contradiction. In the case of valid arguments the information asserted in the conclusion is in some sense already contained in the premises.

Ruling out the assertion of both a proposition and the negation of that proposition is the minimum condition for engaging in rational discourse. If we permit that it is rationally legitimate simultaneously to assert a proposition and to assert its negation, or, which amounts to the same thing, to assert and deny the same proposition, then all rational discussion and argument would break down and become impossible; there would be no distinction between assertion and denial, in which circumstances it is difficult to see how any rational communication is possible at all. Traditional logic has it that if contradictions are permitted, then we cannot rule out *any* proposition whatsoever being true, or to put it another way, any proposition you like is true. Formally this is put by saying that from a contradiction any proposition whatsoever may be derived. Then we would have to agree that all rational discussion aimed at discovering the truth would be pointless.

This is not to say that as a matter of psychological fact people do not hold contradictory propositions or beliefs; they may refuse to give up their contradictory beliefs even when they are pointed out to them. This may be a psychological fact. But it remains the case that if they want to be rational they *ought* to give up and avoid holding contradictory propositions or beliefs. Again we can note that good reasoning is prescriptive or normative, a matter of what we *ought* to do regardless of what anyone in fact does.

2.11 An argument is *invalid* if the conclusion does *not follow from* the premises. The conclusion does not follow from the premises if to assert the premises but deny the conclusion would *not* be a contradiction or inconsistent. With an invalid argument it is possible, because it is neither contradictory nor inconsistent, to assert its premises and deny its conclusion.

2.12 As was said earlier, logic is concerned with argument-forms, not with particular arguments. It is through understanding argument-forms that we come to see why particular valid arguments are valid. Valid arguments are valid because they are instances of valid argument-forms, just as a good apple pie is a good apple pie because it is an instance of a good plan for how an apple pie should be made. The difference is that logic gives, for all practical purposes, a precise account of *all* valid argument-forms, so that if a particular argument is an instance of one of the valid argument-forms, it is a valid argument.

2.13 We need to understand why, for example, the following argument is valid.

All philosophers are thoughtful
Pascal is a philosopher

_____

Pascal is thoughtful

The first thing we need to do is to ignore for the moment the truth or falsity of any of the propositions in the argument. For most people it is intuitively plain that the argument is valid; the conclusion really does follow from the premises. This notion of validity can be put exactly by saying that if the argument is valid then to assert the premises and deny the conclusion would be contradictory. If it is the case that *all* philosophers are thoughtful, then there cannot be a philosopher who is not thoughtful; that includes Pascal since he is a philosopher, so Pascal must be thoughtful.

What we have to see is that we can substitute uniformly whatever propositions we like for the propositions above, provided we keep the same *form*, and we will always have a valid argument. A *substitution-instance* is the insertion in an argument-form of a particular argument. The above argument concerning Pascal is one substitution-instance of a valid argument-form. There are of course many valid argument-forms besides this one.

The form of an argument is really the skeleton of the argument: the underlying shape or structure of it with all the content removed. The form of the above argument is as follows.

All somethings are something
A particular thing is the first something
_____

That particular thing is the second something

Any argument with this argument-form will automatically be a valid argument. Of course we do not, in deciding if something is a valid argument, always need to go through the process of checking if it is an instance of a valid argument-form any more than we need to check the apple pie recipe in order to decide if we are right that the pie tastes like a good apple pie should; it may just be obvious that the pie tastes superb and that an argument is valid; nevertheless the reason an argument is valid is because it is an instance of a valid argument-form.

That the argument above is valid not because of its content but because of its form is made even more obvious if we substitute words which we do not know the meaning of for 'philosopher', 'thoughtful', and 'Pascal'.

All blurgs are flobbs
Grott is a blurg
_____

Grott is a flobb

Naturally we have no idea in this case what blurgs or flobbs are, or what a Grott is. But we still know that if it is the case that *all* blurgs are flobbs, then there cannot be a blurg that is not a flobb, and that includes Grott since a Grott is a blurg, so Grott must be a flobb. The argument is valid.

So the form of this argument is:

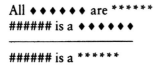

All ♦♦♦♦♦♦ are ******
is a ♦♦♦♦♦♦
_____

is a ******

It is a small step from this to putting the *variable* letters A, B and C to stand in place of ♦♦♦♦♦♦, ******, ######, and thus take the first step towards symbolising arguments (which is just a neater way of doing the same thing), from which we can see that the form of the argument is:

All *A* are *B*
C is an *A*
_____

C is a *B*

So this says that whatever A, B and C are, if *all* A are B, then there cannot be an A that is not a B, and that includes C since it is an A, so C is a B. *Variables* are so called because they stand in place of various expressions (such as 'philosopher', 'thoughtful', and 'Pascal') that can be substituted uniformly as instances of them. By 'uniformly' here is meant that if you put 'philosopher' for 'A', you must put 'philosopher' in all places 'A' occurs in the argument, and so on. This reinforces the idea that valid arguments are valid because of their form, not because of their content. Any particular well-formed expressions whatsoever can be put in place (substituted) for A, B and C, and the argument will always be a valid argument. *All* arguments with that form are valid arguments. All arguments which are cases of some valid argument-form, of which there are many, are valid arguments. Argument-forms as such will be looked at later in the book when we examine basic symbolic logic.

Detailed knowledge of symbolic logic is not necessary to understand the principles of good reasoning or arguing well. Fortunately we can usually see that arguments are good arguments without displaying their bare form. But ultimately it is that form that underpins their being good arguments.

2.14 The talk about form and the talk about contradiction mentioned earlier, can now be tied together. It was said that an argument is valid if the conclusion follows from the premises, in the sense that to assert the premises and deny the conclusion would be a contradiction. It has also been said that an argument is valid because it is an instance of a valid argument-form. These are not two ways in which arguments can be valid, but the same thing said in different ways. Thus any substitution in a valid argument-form will necessarily produce an instance of an argument where to assert the premises and deny the conclusion is a contradiction; in the case of any substitution in a valid argument-form the conclusion will follow from the premises and the argument will be a valid argument.

If we take our example above:

All A are B
C is an A
_____

C is a B

Here we can see that in this, as in all valid argument-forms, whatever we substituted for A, B and C, the conclusion would follow from the premises in that to assert the premises and deny the conclusion would be a contradiction. If 'All A are B', and if 'C is an A', then it would clearly be a contradiction to deny 'C is a B'. To deny the conclusion 'C is a B' on the basis of these premises, which implicitly assert 'C is a B', would be to assert the contradiction 'C is a B and it is not the case that C is a B'. And contradictions are not allowed; they are ruled out of rational discourse, because they are not permissible under any circumstances.

2.15 The following illustrates the same process of seeing why an argument is valid, using another example that is a different form of argument.

If Jack is at the cinema, then Jack is eating ice-cream
Jack is not eating ice-cream
_____

Jack is not at the cinema

Again the first thing to do is to ignore speculation as to the truth or falsity of the propositions in the argument. To assert the premises and deny the conclusion would be a contradiction. The argument asserts that if Jack is at the cinema he eats ice-cream. This means that Jack cannot both be at the cinema and not eat ice-cream. But Jack is not eating ice-cream. From this it follows Jack is not at the cinema, for if he were then he would eat ice-cream.

In the same way as before, we can substitute whatever propositions we like for the propositions above, provided we keep the same *form*, and we will always have a valid argument. The above is a substitution-instance of one of the valid argument-forms.

To show that it is the form of the argument that matters as far as validity is concerned, we can remove the content of the argument to reveal its underlying structure.

If something, then something else
It is not the case that the something else

_____

It is not the case that the first something

Any argument with this form will automatically be valid.

That the argument is valid not because of its content but because of its form can again be illustrated by substituting words whose meaning we do not know.

If Nobes tute, then Larbles floom
Larbles do not floom

_____

Nobes do not tute

We have no idea what Nobes are, or what to tute is; we have no idea what Larbles are, or what flooming is; we have no idea what a Nobe tuting would consist in, or what a Nobe not tuting would consist in. Yet we can say that the argument is valid. The argument asserts that if Nobes tute, then Larbles floom. This means it cannot be the case that Nobes tute and Larbles not floom. But Larbles do not floom. From this it follows that Nobes do not tute, for if they did then Larbles would floom.

So the form of the argument is:

If ——, then ******
not ******

_____

not ——

We can now, as before, put variable letters p and q to stand in place of —— and ******, and symbolise the argument so its form is clear. In the following, 'not-p' and 'not-q' mean the negation of p and q respectively. So that 'not-p' means 'it is not the case that p' – when p is true, not-p is false – and 'not-q' means 'it is not the case that q' – when q is true, not-q is false.

If p, then q
not-q

_____

not-p

The first line says that whatever propositions we substitute for p and q, if p then q. This means it cannot be the case that p and not the case that q. But it is not the case that q. From this it follows that it is not the case that p, since if it were the case that p it would be the case that q.

2.16 If an argument is valid, then the conclusion follows from the premises, in the sense that to assert the premises but deny the conclusion is a contradiction. An argument is valid because it is an instance of a valid argument-form. Any substitution in a valid argument-form will necessarily produce an argument where to assert the premises and deny the conclusion is a contradiction; thus any case of a substitution in a valid argument-form will be one in which the conclusion follows from the premises.

Take again our example above:

If p, then q
not-q

_____

not-p

As in all valid argument-forms, whatever propositions are substituted for p and q, the conclusion would follow from the premises, in that to assert the premises and deny the conclusion would be a contradiction. If it is the case that, 'If p, then q' and 'not-q', then it is clearly a contradiction to deny 'not-p'. To deny 'not-p' on the basis of these premises, which implicitly assert that 'not-p', would be to assert the contradiction 'p is the case and not-p is the case', that is, 'p and not-p'. And, as we know, contradictions are ruled out as the minimum condition for rational discourse: their exclusion is a prerequisite for arguing having any point.

2.17 There is one final way of looking at this notion of validity. The reason for denying that the conclusion of a valid argument is a contradiction is that what is asserted in the conclusion is already contained in the premises, albeit not explicitly asserted. Thus the following argument is clearly valid for that reason.

A and B

B

If you have A and B, then you have B.

2.18 It should be clear now what we mean by an argument being valid, and thus what it means to say that the conclusion follows from the premises. But validity is not enough for good reasoning. It is not sufficient that the conclusion follows from the premises for a set of propositions to constitute a good argument or good reasoning. In good reasoning we are concerned with finding out the *truth* by means of argument. Arguing validly without regard to the truth of the premises only tells us what *follows* given those premises; it does not give a reason for thinking the conclusion true. It only does so if, further to an argument being valid, the premises are also true.

The most important purpose of argument is to *give a reason for thinking the conclusion true*. This is indeed the fundamental way to characterise good arguments. For this to be the case an argument not only has to be *valid* but also the *premises true*. If an argument is valid and the premises true, then it must be the case that the conclusion is true. As before, because the argument is valid we know that to assert the premises and deny the conclusion would be a contradiction. This is not allowed. The same applies, of course, to a valid argument with *true* premises. But in this case it must be the case that the conclusion is true since to deny it would involve a contradiction. If an argument is valid, and the premises true, the truth of the premises is preserved in the conclusion. It is impossible to have a valid argument with true premises and a false conclusion.

An argument that is valid and also has true premises is called a *sound* argument.

2.19 It is, indeed, possible to have every combination of true and false premises, true and false conclusions, and valid and invalid argument, *except* one that is *valid*, has *true* premises and a *false conclusion*.

Here is a complete list of examples of all the possible permutations of true and false premises, true and false conclusions, and validity and invalidity. It should be noted that this is not a complete list by any means of all the forms that arguments can take but is merely a set of examples indicating how true and false premises, true and false conclusions, and valid and invalid argument may be combined. It will be seen that a valid argument with true premises and a false conclusion is not on the list, and this is because it is not possible.

I

VALID. True premises. True conclusion.

All fish have gills	⇒ true
All salmon are fish	⇒ true
———————————	
All salmon have gills	⇒ true

II

VALID. False premises. False conclusion.

All fish have two legs	$\Rightarrow$ false
All two legged creatures are blue	$\Rightarrow$ false
All fish are blue	$\Rightarrow$ false

III

VALID. False premises. True conclusion.

All sparrows are mammals	$\Rightarrow$ false
All hedgehogs are sparrows	$\Rightarrow$ false
All hedgehogs are mammals	$\Rightarrow$ true

IV

INVALID. True premises. True conclusion.

All fish are aquatic	$\Rightarrow$ true
All fish have gills	$\Rightarrow$ true
All things that have gills are aquatic	$\Rightarrow$ true

V

INVALID. True premises. False conclusion.

| All fish are aquatic | $\Rightarrow$ true |
All fish have gills	$\Rightarrow$ true
All fish are mammals	$\Rightarrow$ false

VI

INVALID. False premises. True conclusion.

| All fish have two legs | $\Rightarrow$ false |
All fish are blue	$\Rightarrow$ false
All fish have gills	$\Rightarrow$ true

VII

INVALID. False premises. False conclusion.

| All fish have two legs | $\Rightarrow$ false |
All fish are blue	$\Rightarrow$ false
All fish are mammals	$\Rightarrow$ false

It can be seen from the above list that every combination of true and false premises, true and false conclusions, and validity and invalidity, is possible *except a valid argument with true premises and a false conclusion.*

1   In the case of I, the premises and conclusion are both true, and the conclusion follows from the premises.
2   In the case of II, the premises and conclusion are both false, but the conclusion follows from the premises. If the premises had been true, the conclusion would have been true, but the premises are in fact false.
3   In the case of III, the premises are false and the conclusion true and the conclusion follows from the premises. Although the conclusion is in fact true, and it follows from the premises, the argument does not give a reason for the conclusion owing to the falsity of the premises.
4   In the case of IV, the premises are true and the conclusion is true, but the conclusion does not follow from the premises. Although the premises are true and the conclusion true, the argument does not give a reason for the conclusion owing to its invalidity.
5   In the case of V, the premises are true and the conclusion false, and the conclusion does not follow from the premises.
6   In the case of VI, the premises are false and the conclusion true, and the conclusion does not follow from the premises. Although the conclusion is true, no reason has been given for its truth owing to both the falsity of the premises and the invalidity of the argument.
7   In the case of VII, the premises are false and the conclusion false, and the conclusion does not follow from the premises.

Only the case of I is a good argument; it is a sound argument. In this case, because both the premises are true and the argument valid, a reason has been given for the conclusion being true. Indeed it must be the case that the conclusion is true if the argument has both true premises and is valid.

2.20 It follows from this that if the conclusion of an argument is false, then either the argument is invalid, or, if it is valid, one, at least, of the premises must be false. For if an argument is both valid and the premises true, it must be the case that the conclusion is true.

2.21 Logic, as such, is not concerned with soundness. Logic is concerned with validity: with what can legitimately be said to follow from what. From the point of view of pure logic you can make any assumptions you like and it matters not at all if assumed premises are true or false: its interest is only with what would really *follow* from making those assumptions. *If* we take certain propositions, logic shows us what would follow. Logic cannot, except for tautologies (propositions that must be true and cannot be false) and contradictions (propositions that must be false and cannot be true), tell us which substantive contingent propositions (propositions which may be true or may be false) are true or false. It would be presumptive for logic to do so. (See § 5.21.)

If, for example, we want to know if a certain proposition concerning fleas is true we will have to consult a biologist. We can speculate about fleas all we like and draw out all sorts of implausible, and, it may turn out, false conclusions by perfectly valid reasoning. However, from the point of view of *good reasoning*, we want arguments both to reach true conclusions and to give us a reason for the conclusion being true. If we want an argument to reach true conclusions and give us a reason for the conclusion being true, only true premises must be used and used in valid arguments.

2.22 The threads can now be brought together.

> *Good reasoning consists of using only valid arguments and true premises, for only in this way does an argument give a reason for the conclusion being true.*

3

HOW ARGUMENTS FAIL

3.1 The purpose of this book is not to examine the nature of good reasoning as an end in itself, but rather to instil in the reader a more active way of reading, writing, listening and speaking, when the concern is the quality of arguments. Arguments are a way, a central way, of weighing the value of truth-claims.

We all know that studying a text where arguments are our concern involves a different attitude from reading, say, a novel for relaxation or entertainment. Although there may be an argument embedded in the text of a novel – an argument about how we ought to live our lives, for example – quite often we are, quite rightly, unconcerned with argument. We might simply want to lose ourselves in the story; the criterion we use to assess it will not usually be how good its arguments are, for there may be none, but, say, how it involves us.

When we are studying some subject – history, biology, philosophy – we are often primarily concerned with the quality of arguments. This makes reading (for example) a much more demanding business, one where we have to think things through as we read. As we read we have to think about the quality of the arguments we are being presented with, which is something rather more than simply understanding what is being said; and this essentially involves deciding whether we are being given good reasons for the conclusions the author wishes us to accept.

What this book hopes to do is to present a more *active* way of reading, and a more *self-aware* way of writing (the same applies respectively to listening and speaking), so that you are more effective when it comes to the matter of assessing and constructing arguments. In fact it applies to any form of communication where argument is what matters. The activity consists of highlighting clearly what is involved in being engaged in the assessment and construction of arguments, and what steps one can take to make sure one is so engaged when one should be.

3.2 In the previous chapter we have seen the nature of arguments, and what constitutes good arguments. Although stated implicitly there, it is now important to bring out clearly *how arguments fail*. To have this at the back of the mind, when assessing or producing arguments, is to engage more actively with texts and with what you are writing.

3.3 It is necessary to distinguish between the *objective* failure of arguments and the *person-directed* failure of arguments.

3.4 *Objective failure of arguments*. An argument fails objectively if it does not give a reason for the conclusion being true. There are three ways in which an argument can fail objectively: the argument may be invalid, it may have false premises, or it may be both invalid and have false premises. The first two are each alone sufficient for an argument to fail; the two together are doubly sufficient.

3.5 An argument is invalid if the conclusion does not follow from the premises.

Example

>   All fish are aquatic
>   All fish have gills
>   _____
>   All things that have gills are aquatic

In this case (the case of IV in § 2.19) we can see that there is no contradiction between holding that the premises are true and that the conclusion could be false; therefore the conclusion does not follow from the premises. We should note that the conclusion is true, as indeed are the premises, but because the argument is invalid a reason has not been given for the conclusion being true. The explanation for it being invalid is that just because all *fish* are aquatic and all have gills, it does not follow that there could not be some *other sort of thing* (not a fish) that has gills but is not aquatic. The conclusion would only follow in this argument if the premise were added that *only* fish have gills – but then the question would arise as to whether that were true. But as it stands the argument is invalid.

3.6 If at least one of the premises of an argument is false, then even if the argument is valid, a reason has not been given for thinking the conclusion true.

Example

> All sparrows are mammals
> All hedgehogs are sparrows
> _____
> All hedgehogs are mammals

In this case (the case of III in § 2.19) the conclusion does follow from the premises, but the premises are false. One can say, if an argument is valid and *if* the premises were true, then a reason would have been given for the conclusion being true. But in fact the premises are false so no reason has been given for the conclusion in this argument. Again the conclusion may still be true even if the premises of a valid argument are false, but a reason has not been given for the truth of the conclusion.

3.7 If an argument is valid – that is, the conclusion follows from the premises – but the conclusion is false, then it must be the case that at least one of the premises is false. If the premises had been true, in the case of a valid argument, the conclusion could not have been false. You cannot have a valid argument with true premises and a false conclusion.

3.8 If an argument has both at least one false premise and is invalid, then it fails doubly to give a reason for the conclusion being true.

Example

> All fish have two legs
> All fish are blue
> _____
> All fish have gills

41

In this case (the case of VI in § 2.19) neither are the premises true nor is it valid. The premises are false and the conclusion does not follow from the premises. Although the conclusion is true, a reason has not been given for the conclusion being true.

3.9 *Form.* It is important to emphasise that the validity or invalidity of an argument is determined by its form. Although it is correct to say that an argument is valid because it is an instance of a valid argument-form, it would be incorrect to say that an argument is invalid because it is an instance of *an* invalid argument-form – this is because it may also be an instance of some valid argument-form.

(a) An argument is valid if it is an instance of at least one valid argument-form. An argument is valid if it is an instance of *any* valid argument-form. So all instances of valid argument-forms are valid arguments.

(b) An argument is invalid if it is not an instance of at least one valid argument-form. An argument is invalid if it is not an instance of *any* valid argument-form. So all invalid arguments are instances of no valid argument-form.

An argument is valid if it is an instance of some valid argument-form. An argument is invalid because it is not an instance of any valid argument-form; there is no valid argument-form of which it is an instance.

3.10 *Person-directed failure of arguments.* In this sense an argument is an argument *for* someone. This is not to revive the confusion mentioned earlier between logic and psychology: between an argument being or not being a good argument and it in fact being convincing or not being convincing to someone. It is merely to point out that as arguments are often addressed *to* people, such arguments may fail to give someone a reason for accepting the conclusion, even if they are good arguments in the objective sense and thus in fact do give *a reason* for accepting the conclusion. An argument fails in the person-directed sense if, to the person to whom the argument is addressed, its premises are *unacceptable* or its *validity unclear*, or both the premises are unacceptable and the validity unclear.

3.11 If the premises of a valid argument are unacceptable to someone, even if they are true, *that person* has, in the person-directed sense, not been given a reason to accept the conclusion. In a sense, of course, a perfectly good reason for the conclusion has been given, but a particular person may not have a reason for accepting that the conclusion is true that is a reason *for them*. Suppose I go to the doctor and he tells me I have cancer. I ask him how he knows. He then presents to me a technical argument concerning the tests he has carried out, of the sort he might reasonably address to a medical colleague. Even if the conclusion that I have cancer does indeed follow from the true premises he presents, I might find the premises unacceptable because they are, say, unintelligible to me, and can be seen to be true only by experts. In this person-directed sense of argument failure, the doctor has failed to give *me* a good argument for believing the conclusion to be true.

3.12 What can one do about an argument in which one finds the premises unacceptable? The usual course is to ask for further justification of the premises, so that the original premises are then conclusions of other premises that are acceptable.

3.13 Even if the premises of arguments are true and acceptable and the argument valid, it may still be the case in the person-directed sense that a particular person has not been given a reason for thinking the conclusion true. This may arise because the argument is too complex for a person to follow. In the case of the doctor telling me I have cancer, it may be the case that even if I can see that the premises are true, I might fail to perceive the validity of the argument even if it is valid. I may fail to see that the conclusion follows from those premises even if it does. In the person-directed sense a reason has not been given for my accepting the conclusion as true.

3.14 What can one do about an argument where the validity is unclear? One can seek elucidation of the steps in the argument and try harder to understand better how the conclusion follows from the premises. Of course one will eventually tend toward an end-point in this process in which one cannot elucidate, perhaps by simplifying, the premises and the steps in the argument any further, and a person has tried as hard as they can to understand.

After that nothing more can be done apart from trying again or putting the matter another way. But one hopes that usually it does not come to this. Reasoning is a capacity that is more developed in some people than others, as with any other capacity (such as an ability to run or play tennis) – but it can be improved and nurtured with practice.

3.15 In the case of an argument presented to me by a doctor where to me there are both unacceptable premises and the validity is not apparent, it should be noted that I might believe the premises are true, might believe the argument valid, and might believe the conclusion true, just because I trust that the doctor knows what he is doing. But unless I can see these things for myself, as far as the *argument* is concerned in the person-directed sense, I have not been given a reason to think the conclusion true. Of course I might still accept that what the doctor says is true anyway. This will not be merely because he is an expert or has authority in the relevant area; it is because we think he is capable of constructing good arguments justifying the conclusions he reaches, regardless of whether we can in fact understand them or not, or has reached those conclusions by some path which can be ratified by its implying tacitly or immanently a good argument.

3.16 Understanding how arguments succeed and fail leads us to an active way of reading, writing, speaking, and listening, which for convenience I shall call rational discourse. When we are engaged in rational discourse we need to assess constantly the quality of the arguments: that is, whether a good reason has been given for the conclusion being true. We can do this by bearing in mind two questions.

1   *Is the argument valid?* That is, does the conclusion really follow from the premises as presented, or can the conclusion be denied without contradicting the premises?
2   *Are the premises true?* That is, are any of the propositions from which the conclusion is supposed to follow false?

If an argument fails on either or both of these counts, and the answer to either of the initial questions is 'no', then regardless of the truth of the conclusion: a *reason* has not been given for the conclusion being true, and the argument has failed. To ask these questions as we engage in rational discourse is to engage in it more actively and with more determination to discover the truth. As you are engaged in rational discourse, constantly hold these questions in your mind and apply them to the discourse whose arguments you are judging.

4

DEFINITIONS

4.1 What are definitions for? For the purposes of this discussion we are only concerned with the function of definition in relation to *arguments*. Definitions are given for the purpose of *clarification* of meaning. Arguments are made up of sets of propositions that in turn are made up of words. The propositions can be true or they can be false, and these true and false propositions act as the premises and conclusions of arguments, which can be valid or invalid, sound or unsound.

Truth Stability of meaning of the words constituting propositions is required if such propositions are to be determinately true or false. In addition, that the words in a proposition have a particular meaning will contribute to determining the truth or the falsity of the proposition.

Form Inconsistency in meaning of the terms of an argument can affect its validity. Arguments are valid because they are instances of a valid argument-form. If the meaning of the terms of an argument change in the course of the argument, then the corresponding form of the argument may change to an invalid form and not be an instance of any valid form, so the argument will no longer be valid.

So meaning can affect arguments in two ways:

(a) It will contribute to determining the truth or falsity of propositions.
(b) It will contribute to determining the validity or invalidity of arguments.

As we have seen, arguments fail because they are not instances of any valid argument-form or have false premises, or both of these.

4.2 Suppose John is a painter. Take the following argument:

John shows great enthusiasm in these paintings

The paintings indicate the inspiration of God

Unless we know that the original meaning of 'enthusiasm' is 'inspired by God' (from the Greek '*en*' meaning 'in' and '*theos*' meaning 'God'), we would be puzzled as to why the conclusion followed from the premise. The modern meaning of the word 'enthusiasm' is usually something like 'zealous' or 'ardent', with no implication that God is involved at all.

4.3 *Form.* The argument in § 4.2 *appears* to have the form:

John shows great X in these paintings

The paintings indicate X

The trouble is that the apparent X in the premise might not mean the same as X in the conclusion. Thus the argument would in this case be invalid, for the form of the argument would now *really* be the following.

John shows great Y in these paintings

The paintings indicate X

If the word 'enthusiasm' (X) in the premise means 'inspired by God' then the argument is valid. If the word 'enthusiasm' (Y) means simply 'zealous' then the argument is invalid. Notice it is still the form and not the content that determines whether the argument is valid or not. It is not the particular meaning of the terms that matters in settling the validity or invalidity of an argument, but whether a term is used *consistently* (that is, with *consistent meaning*) between the premise and conclusion and preserves a valid form.

4.4 *Truth.* If John is said to exhibit 'enthusiasm' with the meaning *X*, it may in fact be false of him. In the case that it is false of John we would have an argument with a false premise, but one which is valid.

4.5 *Form and truth.* It could be the case that 'enthusiasm' with meaning *Y* is false of John, in which case the argument fails doubly: it is invalid (a failure of form) and has a false premise (a failure in having at least one premise that is not true).

4.6 This brings home the importance of being clear about what we mean by the words we use when assessing the truth of propositions and validity, and therefore the importance of meaning for arguments. If there is uncertainty over the meaning of words used in an argument, we will be at a loss as to how to assess it and determine whether it is a good argument or not. If we are in doubt, a way to settle the matter is to ask for a definition of the word whose meaning is unclear.

The important thing here in the case of arguments is not the truth or accuracy of the definition, but what the meaning of the word in question *is*: that the word is given *a* determinate meaning. This is because only in that way can we assess the two vital elements involved in arguments: the truth of their premises and their validity.

4.7 In most cases there is no requirement for definitions to determine the meaning of words and hence of propositions. We are all clear about what the words mean, or at least the meaning is clear enough for the sake of the arguments in which the words are deployed. Quite how this comes about and what it amounts to is a matter of dispute between philosophers, and need not concern us here; for it is just a fact that, however it happens, in the vast majority of cases we have no difficulty in knowing what words and propositions mean.

4.8 Where there is doubt as to the meaning of words, the meaning can be clarified by way of a definition of that word. There are two ways in which this can be done. One is by giving the *intension* of the word and the other is by giving the *extension* of the word.

4.9 *Intension.* In this case we usually give the meaning of the word by means of a set of other words that does not use the word being defined. Thus we might say:

fish =df. creature that lives in the water and has gills

4.10 *Extension.* In this case we either point to an instance of the sort of thing we mean (an ostensive definition) or we list the things that fall under the meaning of the word.

fish =df. look, one of *these* (pointing at a fish)

or

fish =df. carp, herring, cod, salmon . . .

4.11 Either the intension or extension are ways of indicating the meaning of words. Which we choose will depend upon the circumstances and what it is we are trying to define. In the case of colours, for example, it has been claimed that because they are simple – that is not made up of parts found anywhere else – there is no way of indicating what is meant by red except through an encounter with an example of it. This is called giving an *ostensive* definition. Complex things can be defined by ostension, but also by referring to their constituent characteristics. Thus:

unicorn =df. a fictional creature, looking like a horse, but with a single long straight horn sticking out of the front of its head

4.12 *Necessary and sufficient conditions.* A classic way of defining something by *intension* is through the use of necessary and sufficient conditions. A thing can be defined by giving both the necessary and sufficient conditions for it to be the sort (or kind) of thing it is. This is not to make any commitment as to whether that sort of thing exists (*that* it is) but to give a condition or set of conditions that pick that thing out from all other sorts of thing (*what* it is). In defining something in this way we are saying what is – what has to be the case – for that thing to be the sort of thing it is.

Traditionally this is spoken of as characterising the *essence* of a thing. The essential properties of a thing contrast with its *accidental* properties, which are neither necessary nor sufficient for the thing to be the sort of thing it is. The accidental features of a thing are irrelevant to defining it and picking it out as the sort of thing it is as opposed to its being any other sort of thing. Thus, if we were trying to define a human being, we would not include as a necessary or a sufficient condition 'having red hair'. This is because it is an accidental feature: something can be a human being without having red hair, and something can have red hair without being a human being. It is not a part of the essence of what it is to be a human being. Often what the necessary and sufficient conditions refer to are the features, properties or qualities of a sort of thing.

Another way of putting this is to say that we are looking for some condition or set of conditions that *all and only* those sorts of thing have in common.

Suppose F is a necessary condition for x.
If some thing is an x then it must have feature F.
That is, any thing that is x will have feature F. It is necessary for some thing to be x that it has feature F. Therefore some thing cannot be x without having feature F.

Suppose F is a sufficient condition for x.
If some thing has the feature F then it must be x.
That is, any thing that has feature F will be x. It is sufficient for some thing to have feature F for it to be x. Therefore some thing is x if it has feature F.

However, a feature F can be a necessary condition but not a sufficient condition for x, and F can be a sufficient condition but not a necessary condition for x. If a feature is both necessary and sufficient we have defined x and distinguished it from all other sorts of things. In a sense therefore necessary and sufficient conditions work in opposite directions to focus on the thing we are defining.

When F is a necessary condition for x: if we have x we have F.
When F is a sufficient condition for x: if we have F we have x.

Example

Being in the Government is a necessary (but not a sufficient) condition for being Prime Minister.

Being Prime Minister is a sufficient (but not a necessary) condition for being in the Government.

Example

Being an article of footwear is a *necessary*, but *not* a sufficient condition, for being a sandal.

Why is the condition necessary? It is because some thing cannot be a sandal unless it is an article of footwear. Why is the condition not sufficient? It is because some thing can be an article of footwear without being a sandal. A boot or a shoe is an article of footwear.

Example

Being a sandal is a *sufficient* condition, but *not* a necessary condition, for being an article of footwear.

Why is the condition sufficient? It is because if some thing is a sandal it must be an article of footwear. Why is the condition not necessary? It is because some thing can be an article of footwear without being a sandal. A boot or a shoe is an article of footwear.

Let us define a sandal by giving both necessary and sufficient conditions.

> sandal = df. an article of footwear originally with a substantially open upper

If this definition is correct, then it picks out sandals from all other things by identifying those features taken together that all sandals have, and only sandals have, in common. No thing that is a sandal does not have them (so a necessary condition), and everything that does have them is a sandal (so a sufficient condition).

Another way of explaining this is by a kind of formula saying that if we have the correct necessary and sufficient condition F, then something is x, *if and only if* it meets this condition. The necessary condition provides the *only if* part of this, and the sufficient conditions provide the *if* part of this. Thus we might explain it by writing:

Necessary condition: *x* only if *F*

$\Rightarrow$ Necessary and sufficient: *x* if and only if *F*

Sufficient condition: *x* if *F*

Testing definitions given by necessary and sufficient conditions

The nature of necessary and sufficient conditions gives the clue as to how they should be tested for correctness. For a definition to be correct it must provide both the necessary and sufficient conditions. If it fails to provide either the necessary or sufficient conditions, or both, the definition has failed: it has failed to pick out a certain sort of thing as distinct from all other sorts of thing.

If *F* is a necessary condition for *x* then there can be no thing that is *x* that does not have *F*. If we can think of *x* that does not have *F*, then we know *F* cannot be a necessary condition for *x*. If *F* is a sufficient condition for *x* then there can be no thing that has *F* that is not *x*. If we can think of a thing that has *F* but is not *x*, then we know *F* cannot be a sufficient condition for *x*.

Is *F* a necessary condition for *x*? Test: can there be *x* that does not have *F*? Yes: then *F* is not a necessary condition for *x*.

Is *F* a sufficient condition for *x*? Test: can there be a thing that has *F* that is not *x*? Yes: then *F* is not a sufficient condition for *x*.

A failure in either test or both of them means that we have not given a satisfactory definition of the thing we attempted to define.

Multiple conditions

Usually in defining some thing we find that more than one condition is involved. If there are several conditions [*F G H*] that define *x*, they are said to be *each necessary* and *jointly sufficient*. Therefore [*F G H*] is said to give the necessary and sufficient conditions for *x*.

If [*F G H*] gives the correct definition then:

> Some thing cannot be *x* if it is lacking *any* of [*F G H*]: the conditions are each necessary. Some thing that has *all* of [*F G H*] must be *x*: the conditions are jointly sufficient.

> So together [*F G H*] is both necessary and sufficient for *x*.

The definition is tested for correctness as before.

> Can there be an *x* that lacks *any* of the conditions [*F G H*]? If there is, then we have not given the necessary conditions for *x*.
> Can there be a thing that has *all* the conditions [*F G H*] but is not *x*? If there is, then we have not given the sufficient conditions for *x*.

If the proposed definition fails in either of these ways or both – that is, we have failed to provide either the necessary or sufficient conditions, or both – we have failed to give a definition of *x*.

Example

> fish = df. lives in water and breathes using gills

Here we have two conditions:

> *F* = lives in water
> *G* = breathes using gills

There cannot be a fish that either does not live in water or breathes using gills. Therefore the conditions are each necessary. If either were not necessary, there would be a fish that either did not live in the water or have gills, or both. So to test the definition we look for some thing that is a fish, but does not satisfy conditions *F* or *G*, or both, and if we find some thing the definition has failed.

There cannot be a thing that lives in water and breathes using gills that is not a fish. Therefore the conditions are sufficient. If they were not sufficient there would be a thing that both lives in the water and breathes using gills, but is not a fish. So to test the definition we look for some thing that satisfies the conditions F and G, but is not a fish, and if we find some thing the definition has failed.

> The conditions F and G are each necessary and jointly sufficient to define a fish. Therefore they are necessary and sufficient to define a fish.

Other important uses for necessary and sufficient conditions

Necessary and sufficient conditions can be used to give definitions of anything that is a sort or kind of thing. It does not have to be an object such as a physical object like a chair or a horse. It might be an institution like 'democracy', or a moral concept like 'justice', or a descriptive term like 'art'.

In addition necessary and sufficient conditions are important in making distinctions when we talk about the world. Necessary and sufficient conditions are a way of talking about the causes of things: water and oxygen are each necessary and jointly sufficient to cause rust. We can apply them to historical events: it could be argued that the First World War was a necessary, but not a sufficient, condition for the Second World War; for that a charismatic leader like Hitler needed to appear in Germany at the right time. Being at a concert is normally a sufficient condition for my hearing the music, but it is not a necessary one, for I might hear it on the radio; whereas having a ticket is normally a necessary condition for hearing a live concert as a member of the audience, but not a sufficient one because I might decide not to go.

4.13 Some philosophers deny that in many, perhaps even all, cases such essential definitions are either required or possible as far as coming to understand the meaning of a word and its having a meaning is concerned. The suggestion here is that there is usually not one unique set of properties or features that pick out all and only things of the same sort, but various overlapping features (like a family resemblance) between those things that mean they get grouped together as the same sort or connected. But these speculations would take us beyond the scope of this book. We can be sure of one thing however: unless we can have a stable idea of what words mean in some way, we would be at a loss to know if arguments are good or not. If we do not know what propositions, made up of words, *mean* we could not hope to assess the merits of arguments involving those propositions.

4.14 *Extreme inconsistency.* Arguments are valid because they are instances of valid argument-forms. That an argument is an instance of a valid argument-form partly depends on terms in the argument being used consistently. Take the following valid argument-form where p and q stand in place of particular propositions.

Example

> If p then q
> not-q
> _____
>
> not-p

The validity of this argument depends on maintaining the pattern:

> If ##### then ******
> not-******
> _____
>
> not-#####

Suppose we constructed an instance of this valid argument-form as follows.

> If Jack is at the cinema, then Jack is eating ice-cream
> Jack is not eating ice-cream
> _____
>
> Jack is not at the cinema

Here:

> p = Jack is at the cinema
> q = Jack is eating ice-cream

not-*q* = Jack is not eating ice-cream
not-*p* = Jack is not at the cinema

This argument is valid because it is an instance of a valid argument-form.

Suppose now we constructed an example with a variation:

Jack is at the cinema, then Jack is eating ice-cream
Jack is not buying ice-cream

_____

Jack is not at the cinema

Remember the issue here is not the truth of the conclusion, but whether an argument has been given for the conclusion in this instance. Setting aside the matter of the truth of the premises for the moment, the question then is whether the argument is valid. It is clearly invalid. The conclusion does not follow from the premises. It is possible for the premises to be true and the conclusion false, therefore the argument cannot be valid.

Another way of putting this is to say that the argument is invalid because it is not an instance of any valid argument-form. Here:

p = Jack is at the cinema
q = Jack is eating ice-cream
not-*r* = Jack is not buying ice-cream
not-*p* = Jack is not at the cinema

So the invalid form of the argument is:

If *p* then *q*
not-*r*

_____

not-*p*

This is not a valid argument-form. An argument is only valid if it is an instance of a valid argument-form; since this is not in this case an instance of any valid argument-form it cannot be a valid argument.

What has happened here in a sense is that we have been inconsistent in our use of terms. If 'Jack is not buying ice-cream' *meant* 'Jack is not eating ice-cream', then we would be back to the first example and have a valid argument. Of course it does not mean the same because it is perfectly possible, and thus consistent (not contradictory), to say both that Jack is eating ice-cream and Jack is not buying ice-cream – thus 'not-r' is not the negation of p – he may after all be given an ice-cream or steal it.

4.15 The central issue here, as far as assessing whether arguments are good or bad is concerned, is that we need to know the meaning of their terms in order to determine (a) the meaning of the premises, and (b) if the terms are being used consistently between premise and conclusion. We need to know the meaning of the premises in order to assess the truth of the premises. We need to know if the terms are used consistently in order to assess the validity of the arguments; if terms are used inconsistently then the argument may be invalid. Both these things are relevant in judging arguments good or bad since arguments fail either because of their false premises or their invalidity, or both.

5

BASIC SYMBOLIC LOGIC

5.1 We have clearly seen that the *validity* of good arguments is a matter of their *form*.

5.2 Logic is interested in identifying the sort of valid argument-forms there can be: it is concerned with what it is correct to say follows from what. In this sense it is not concerned with particular truths, but with determining, if you assert something, what would follow from what you assert. It sets out to display the basic valid forms of reasoning, on the view that all complex forms of valid reasoning are built up from the basic forms. Logic is only interested in those elements in ordinary language that are relevant to questions of validity. It extracts from ordinary language only those aspects of the language that determine validity. What it presents is a stripped down version of ordinary language – its skeleton – for the purpose of assessing valid reasoning.

5.3 This is why logic uses *symbols*, a special notation. In this way it is made clear that it is form that matters in relation to validity and not content. It is because logic only needs to deal with the form of arguments to determine issues of validity, and validity is its only concern, that it uses symbols to stand in place of elements in ordinary language. It does not use, and does not have to use, particular propositions like 'Sarah is standing on her head' in discussing validity, that is, the question of what follows from what. The content of propositions is irrelevant. This is sometimes put by saying that logic is extensional. Thus in displaying the form of an argument in order to determine its validity, symbols are used because it does not matter about the content. Symbols are also neater and clearer. If a particular argument is valid or invalid it is because of its form, not its particular content. If an argument is valid it is an instance of at least one valid argument-form that would be valid whatever propositions it was made up of. If an argument is invalid it is an instance of no valid argument-form.

5.4 So for example '*p*' gets used to stand in place of any proposition you like, and '&' gets used to stand for 'and' insofar as the use of 'and' is relevant to the issue of validity. Thus letters *p, q, r,* . . . are used to stand in place of propositions. These letters are called *variables* because they can stand in place of various propositions. Take the propositions:

Sarah is standing on her head

Fish have bad tempers

These can be compounded into the proposition:

Sarah is standing on her head *and* fish have bad tempers

From the point of view of those issues of validity that interest logic, and treating of propositions as a whole, this compound proposition may be fully represented by the following:

p stands in place of 'Sarah is standing on her head'

q stands in place of 'Fish have bad tempers'

and then writing it as:

p & *q*

This is the form of the compound proposition, and that is all that matters to logic. So this can now stand in place of all propositions with that form. The content is drained out of it. The content is irrelevant, and symbols make sure we are not distracted by the content. There is no more mystery to using symbols in logic than that.

5.5 We can summarise by saying that symbols are used in logic because:

(a) They are neater, clearer and easier to work with.
(b) They make it obvious that form alone and not the possibly distracting content is relevant to validity, and hence to logic.

5.6 There are two ways of making sure of the formal validity of argument: (a) Truth-tables and (b) Rules of Deduction. These two ways are really the same method applied in different ways. Truth-tables become cumbersome to use for long arguments; in such cases Rules of Deduction are more efficient. However, truth-tables are essential because they are basic to formal logic. Whatever the Rules of Deduction they are ultimately validated by reference to the truth-tables. What will be presented here is often called classical logic.

5.7 *Rules of Deduction.* These are presented in two ways in modern logic.

1   Rules of Inference
2   Natural Deduction

Both of these will be presented here. From the point of view of basic logic they are essentially two ways of doing the same thing: they are ways of showing which arguments are valid and which invalid. They do this in rather different ways by presenting a list of permitted valid moves in arguments. What is valid and what is invalid does not differ substantially between the two methods. Any argument that has all permitted, valid, moves is valid. Any non-valid argument has one or more non-permitted, invalid, move.

5.8 *Truth-tables.* As will be seen in more detail later, the method is first to give the value *true* or the value *false* to each of the propositions in an argument. Then true/false values are read off in turn depending on the way the propositions are connected, leading to a true/false for the argument as a whole. In short the overall true/false value of a complex is determined by, and dependent upon, the true/false value of the simpler parts. This will become clearer with the examples below.

5.9 *Rules of Inference.* The method here is only to use steps in the argument that are known to be valid. If each of the steps is valid, then in sum the argument overall must be valid. Similarly, when each link in a chain is strong then the chain overall is just that strong. Conversely, if the chain is faulty then this is because at least one of the links is faulty. In the case of arguments they are either valid or invalid, and nothing in between (so not weaker or stronger, rather either broken or intact). If an argument is invalid, then it has at least one invalid step.

5.10 *Propositional logic and predicate logic.* There are two fundamental parts to modern logic: *propositional logic* and *predicate logic*. These are not two different sorts of logic. Rather, predicate logic is merely an extension of propositional logic, and allows the analysis of arguments not open to propositional logic. Propositional logic can deal only with arguments insofar as they are considered as combinations of *whole* propositions. Predicate logic allows us to look *within* the propositions themselves and take them apart.

5.11 *Operators.* These are sometimes called *logical connectives*; but since some of them do not connect anything, *operators* is the better term because they all 'operate on' or do things to propositions. In talking of operators we are concerned here with symbols with constant meaning that form the variables, the simplest propositions, $p, q, r, \ldots$ into complexes. In just this way the operator '&' forms the complex p & q. The constant meaning of the operators is determined by the truth-tables.

5.12 *Propositional logic.* There are five operators in propositional logic.

Symbol	Meaning	Name
~	not	negation
&	and	conjunction
v	and/or	disjunction
→	if . . . then . . .	conditional
≡	if and only if (iff)	biconditional

If the operators are put with propositions we have the following results.

Symbols	Meaning	Example
$\sim p$	not-p	*not*-(the cat is black)

$p \mathbin{\&} q$	p and q	the cat is black *and* the dog is brown
$p \vee q$	p or q	the cat is black *or* the dog is brown (or both)
$p \rightarrow q$	if p then q	*if* the cat is black *then* the dog is brown
$p \equiv q$	p if and only if q	the cat is black *if and only if* the dog is brown

5.13 One more symbol needs to be referred to. The three dots ∴ mean 'therefore'.

5.14 *Brackets.* Brackets are used in logic because they mark the 'scope' or limits of the operators. Otherwise the meaning of the whole expression would be unclear. By using brackets it is possible to 'nest' some expressions inside others. Brackets get used for the same reason commonly in arithmetic and algebra. They are necessary for clarity of meaning with regard to the scope of the operators in arithmetic such as the 'plus' + sign and the 'multiplication' x sign. Take for example this.

$$5 + 6 \times 4 =$$

This is ambiguous. It could mean either of the following, and the answers in each case are quite different.

$$(5 + 6) \times 4 = 44$$
$$5 + (6 \times 4) = 29$$

The brackets make it clear what the sum is by making it clear how the arithmetical operators apply.

In the same way in logic the following expression is ambiguous.

$$p \rightarrow q \vee r$$

It could mean either of the following, and whether the argument is valid or not could depend on which is meant.

$$(p \rightarrow q) \vee r$$

This says: 'you have "if p then q" or you have "r", or both'.

$$p \rightarrow (q \vee r)$$

This says: 'if you have "p" then you have "q or r, or both"'.

5.15 Simple propositions can be built up into complex propositions.

$$(\sim(p \ \& \ q) \vee q) \rightarrow (p \equiv q)$$

This, it so happens, uses all the operators of propositional logic by way of illustration. Do not worry about whether it makes sense. It would read something like the following if we substituted:

p = the cat is black
q = the dog is brown

if (*not*-(the cat is black *and* the dog is brown) *or* the dog is brown) *then* (the cat is black *if and only if* the dog is brown)

5.16 *Well-Formed Formulae (wff).* In logic, just as in ordinary language, it is possible to put expressions together in such a way that the result is nonsense because it is seriously ungrammatical. True nonsense should be distinguished from statements that are commonly called nonsense but are in fact merely false in a silly way, such as, 'Cows love to read Plato while jumping the moon'. Thus true nonsense would be: 'A the solely so back at'. So certain combinations of symbols in logic are nonsense in the same way, such as: $\rightarrow pq \vee \& p \equiv$.

5.17 *Defining the operators using truth-tables.* Each operator is defined by constructing a truth-table, that is, by considering what would be the case if all the possible combinations of true and false are given to the simple propositions p and q.

Such complex expressions are said to be *truth-functional*, because the truth of the whole expression is dependent on (is a function of) the truth of its constituent parts. The overall truth-value of the whole expression is determined by the truth-value of the propositions making it up.

Negation

not-p

$\sim p$

p	$\sim p$
T	F
F	T

When p is true, not-p is false, and when p is false, not-p is true.

If p is true, then the negation of p must be false. If it is the case that p, then it-is-not-the-case-that p must be false.

If something is true, then the opposite of that truth must be false.

Conjunction

p and q

p & q

p	q	p & q
T	T	T
T	F	F
F	T	F
F	F	F

When p and q are both true, then their conjunction is true, otherwise it is false.

The whole conjunction of p and q is true if and only if both p and q are true; if one or both is false, then the conjunction is false.

Disjunction

p or *q*

p v *q*

p	*q*	*p* v *q*
T	T	T
T	F	T
F	T	T
F	F	F

When *p* and *q* are both true, or either is true, the disjunction of *p* and *q* is true, otherwise it is false.

The whole disjunction of *p* and *q* is true if they are both true and if either is true, but if they are both false then the disjunction is false.

Conditional

If *p* then *q*

p → *q*

p	*q*	*p* → *q*
T	T	T
T	F	F
F	T	T
F	F	T

When *p*, the antecedent, is true or when it is false, so long as the consequent *q* is not false, then the implication is true.

The whole implication is true except when *p* is true and *q* is false.

A special note needs to be added about the conditional. The → sign is not meant to capture all the meanings that different conditionals have in ordinary language. Hence it is called a *material conditional*. It does not and is not meant to mark a *connection* between the antecedent and the conclusion. The ramifications of this are too complex to go into here. Suffice it to say that the aim of the material conditional, as captured in its truth-table, is not to cover the range of ways conditionals differ and are used in ordinary language but what they have in common, namely, that if the antecedent is true and the consequent false then the whole is false. What the truth-table for the conditional rules out is the move from the true to the false.

Biconditional

p if and only if *q*

$p \equiv q$

p	q	$p \equiv q$
T	T	T
T	F	F
F	T	F
F	F	T

When *p* and *q* are both true or both false the biconditional is true, otherwise it is false.

The whole biconditional is true if and only if *p* and *q* have the same truth-value.

All five operators

It is possible to summarise the truth-tables for all the operators in the following way.

p	$\sim p$
T	F
F	T

p	q	$p \,\&\, q$	$p \vee q$	$p \rightarrow q$	$p \equiv q$
T	T	T	T	T	T
T	F	F	T	F	F
F	T	F	T	T	F
F	F	F	F	T	T

5.18 *Testing arguments using truth-tables.* We can now use these truth-tables to test two arguments: one valid and one invalid.

A valid argument

Denying the consequent (*Modus Tollens*):

$$((p \rightarrow q) \,\&\, \sim q) \rightarrow \sim p$$

The explanation here is that if p implies q, and you do not have q, then you cannot have p, because if you did have p you would have q.

This argument is valid whatever propositions you consistently substitute for p and q.

That this is so can be shown by using truth-tables to analyse the argument. If the argument is valid there will be no possible substitution of true or false propositions that will render the whole false. One tests each part, reading off the value true or false from the truth-tables depending on the truth-value of the constituent propositions, and taking account of the scope introduced by the brackets, from which one eventually comes up with a truth-value for the whole. Every possible combination of truth and falsity is tried. One works, so to speak, from the outside in. It will be seen that the whole expression always comes out true.

If one has an argument with two propositions, p and q, then there are four possible combinations of true and false values that can be given to p and q.

1   p is true (T) and q is true (T)
2   p is true (T) and q is false (F)

3   p is false (F) and q is true (T)
4   p is false (F) and q is false (F)

Taking case (1) where p is T and q is T as an example:

First step   On the first row assign the truth-values to p and q to each of the instances of p and q. In the first case p is true (T), and q is true (T). This must be done consistently, so that if p is T in one instance, it must be given the same truth-value T in all other instances where it occurs. The same applies to q.

Second step   On the next row down assign the correct truth-value according to the truth-table of T or F for the closest operator to p and q using the values given in the previous row. So, in the example:

> If p is T and q is T, then $(p \rightarrow q)$ is T
> If q is T then $\sim q$ is F

Third step   On the next row down assign the correct truth-value according to the truth-tables of T or F for the next closest operators using the values given in the previous row. So in the example:

> If $(p \rightarrow q)$ is T, and $\sim q$ is F, then $((p \rightarrow q) \& \sim q)$ is F
> If p is T, then $\sim p$ is F

Fourth step   On the next row down assign the correct truth-values according to the truth-tables of T or F for the next closest operators using the values given in the previous row. So for example:

> If $((p \rightarrow q) \& \sim q)$ is F, and $\sim p$ is F, then $(((p \rightarrow q) \& \sim q) \rightarrow \sim p)$ is T

In fact the overall expression always comes out true (T). One shows this by repeating the truth-table test for every possible permutation of T and F for p and q.

In diagrammatic form the four-stage truth-table analysis, for all four possible permutations of p and q, will look as follows below. It will be noticed, then, that in this case the argument always comes out with the final (as highlighted) value of T whatever the initial assignment of values to p and q. The argument is therefore valid.

1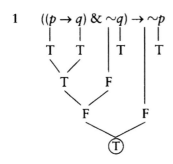

2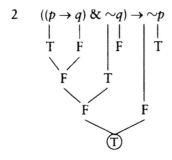

3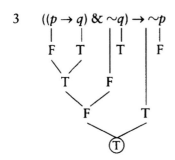

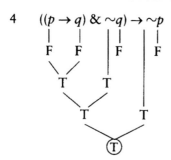

In more compact form, these four possible assignments of values for p and q can be written as follows:

$((p \rightarrow q) \,\&\, \sim q) \rightarrow \sim p$

T T T F FT Ⓣ FT

T F F F TF Ⓣ FT

F T T F FT Ⓣ TF

F T F T TF Ⓣ TF

By assessment in the truth-tables of the penultimate step in each row, that is, combining the result of the fourth column and eighth column – respectively from top to bottom, F → F, F → F, F → T, T → T – giving the result in the final seventh column, it can be seen that the truth-value of the whole is always T and never F. Therefore the argument is valid.

An invalid argument

Affirming the consequent:

$((p \rightarrow q) \,\&\, q) \rightarrow p$

The explanation here is that it is mistakenly claimed that if p implies q, and you have q, then you must have p. The first part of the argument says only that if you have p you have q, but that does not mean that if you have q you must have p or cannot have q without p.

This argument is invalid because there is at least one consistent substitution of truth-values for *p* and *q* where the whole expression comes out false.

That this is so can again be shown by using truth-tables to analyse the argument. If the argument is invalid there will be a possible substitution of true or false propositions that will render the whole false. As before, one tests each part, reading off the value true or false from the truth-tables depending on the truth-value of the constituent propositions, and taking account of the scope introduced by the brackets, from which one eventually comes up with a truth-value for the whole. Every possible combination of truth and falsity is tried. It will be seen that the whole expression *can* come out false.

$$((p \rightarrow q) \& q) \rightarrow p$$

```
T  T  T  T  T  T  T
T  F  F  F  F  T  T
F  T  T  T  T (F) F
F  T  F  F  F  T  F
```

By assessment in the truth-tables of the penultimate step in each row, that is, combining the result of the fourth column and seventh column, giving the result in the final sixth column, it can be seen that in the third row – T → F – the truth-value of the whole can be F and not always T. Therefore the argument is invalid.

5.19 *Establishing invalidity.* The failure to *establish* that a given argument is valid does not show that it is invalid. It may be invalid, but it might just be that we have simply not found the way in which the conclusions can be deduced from the premises using only valid steps. The way to show that an argument is invalid is to show that there is some assignment of truth-values to the propositions that make it up, such that the conclusion can be false while the premises are true. For we know that if it is possible to get from true premises to a false conclusion an argument cannot be valid, therefore it must be invalid.

This fits exactly our intuitive notion of validity already discussed: think of a way in which the conclusion could be false while the premises are true. What we are being asked to accept could be false while the evidence on which we are asked to accept it could still be true. In which case the conclusion (what we are being asked to accept) does not follow from the premises (the evidence on which we are being asked to accept it).

It is possible to show invalidity without constructing the whole truth-table for the argument. Take the following invalid argument:

	1.	$A \rightarrow B$	(premise)
	2.	B	(premise)
$\therefore$	3.	A	(conclusion)

If there is some assignment of truth-values that can make the conclusion 3 false while the premises 1 and 2 are true, then we know that the argument is invalid regardless of what other assignments of truth-values can be made. The important point to note here in assigning the truth-values – as in all cases – is that the assignment is *uniform*. If A takes the value true or the value false in the premises it must do so in the conclusion, and the same applies to B. So suppose the conclusion A is false. Is there a way, guided by the truth-tables, in which the premises can also be true? Is there a way of getting from true premises to a false conclusion? The answer is that there is.

A = false
B = true

	1.	false $\rightarrow$ true	= true	(premise)
	2.	true	= true	(premise)
$\therefore$	3.	false	= false	(conclusion)

Thus the premises can be true while the conclusion is false, so the argument is invalid.

$((A \rightarrow B) \& B) \rightarrow A$
F T T T T Ⓕ F

The individual propositions in the argument, A and B, are given truth-values, and the truth-value of their combination with the operators → and & is given by referring to the truth-tables. This shows that one line in the truth-table is such that the conclusion is false while the premises are true. The argument is therefore invalid.

5.20 All this concurs with what we have said about what it is for an argument to be valid: a valid argument is one in which it is not possible for the premises to be true and the conclusion false.

5.21 Propositions can be divided into three sorts.

1   Tautological: e.g. (p v ~p)
2   Contradictory: e.g. (p & ~p)
3   Contingent: e.g. (p & q)

If these are tested by truth-tables, tautologies always come out true, contradictories always come out false, and contingencies sometimes come out true and sometimes false. This can be put another way. Tautologies are always true because they are true whatever propositions are substituted in them. Contradictories are always false because they are false whatever propositions are substituted in them. Contingencies are sometimes true and sometimes false depending on the propositions we substitute for them. Thus:

Tautology:

(p v ~p)

(either it is raining (p) or it is not raining (~p)) – is always true

Contradiction:

(p & ~p)

(it is both raining (p) and not raining (~p)) – is always false

Contingent:

(p & q)

(it is raining (p) and the cat is on the mat (q)) – is sometimes true and sometimes false

Philosophically it is often argued that tautologies and contradictions can tell us nothing substantive about the world precisely because they are respectively always true and always false, regardless of what propositions are substituted in them – the tautological statement that it is 'Either raining or not raining', because it covers every possibility, is hardly much help in deciding whether one should take an umbrella or not. It is further argued that only contingent truths can give us substantive truths. Since logic alone can only determine the truth-value of tautologies and contradictions and it cannot determine the truth-value of contingent propositions, it cannot legitimately decide any substantive truths about the world.

5.22 *Assessing arguments using rules of inference.* Truth-tables become unwieldy for long or complex arguments in deciding whether arguments are valid or not. A more convenient method is using only steps that are known to be valid, and in this way one knows that the whole argument made up of those steps is valid. Conversely any argument that is invalid will contain an invalid step (not all valid steps). But it must be noted that the legitimacy of the method using rules of inference is ultimately derived from their vindication in the truth-tables.

The question then is: can the conclusion be derived from the premises using only steps known to be valid? If it can, then the conclusion can be validly drawn from the premises. The argument is valid.

5.23 *Validity and proof.* A *valid* argument is one where the conclusion *follows* from the premises, regardless of whether the premises are true. A *proof* requires this and more. A conclusion is proved when the conclusion follows validly from *true* premises. It is sometimes said then that the argument is not merely valid but *sound*.

5.24 Here then are nine basic rules of inference. They can all be shown to be valid by the truth-tables.

1   *Modus Ponens* (MP)

$p \rightarrow q$

p

$\therefore q$

2 *Modus Tollens* (MT)

$p \rightarrow q$

$\sim q$

$\therefore \sim p$

3 *Hypothetical Syllogism* (HS)

$p \rightarrow q$

$q \rightarrow r$

$\therefore p \rightarrow r$

4 *Disjunctive Syllogism* (DS)

$p \vee q$

$\sim p$

$\therefore q$

5 *Simplification* (Simp)

$p \,\&\, q$

$\therefore p$

6 *Constructive Dilemma* (CD)

$(p \rightarrow q) \,\&\, (r \rightarrow s)$

$p \vee r$

$\therefore q \vee s$

7 *Conjunction* (Conj)

p

q

$\therefore p \,\&\, q$

8 *Absorption* (Abs)

$p \rightarrow q$

$\therefore p \rightarrow (p \,\&\, q)$

9   *Addition* (Add)

p

$\therefore p \lor q$

5.25 Any substitution-instance of an argument in a valid argument-form, such as one of the nine rules of inference, is therefore a valid argument. An example using rule (5) Simplification (Simp).

$A=$ I have an apple
$B=$ I have an orange

Substituting A for p and B for q.

$A \,\&\, B$
$\therefore A$

In words this might roughly read as follows.

I have an apple and I have an orange
_____

Therefore, I have an apple

The derivation using the rules of inference would be as follows.

1. $A \,\&\, B$ $\therefore A$
2. A 1, Simp

5.26 We can substitute sequences of any length – chunks of well-formed formulae – provided we do so uniformly in valid arguments, and they will then also be valid arguments.
Let:

$(A \lor B) = p$
$(C \rightarrow (D \,\&\, E)) = q$

Substituting in the valid rule of inference (1) *Modus Ponens* (MP):

$$p \rightarrow q$$
$$p$$
$$\therefore q$$

gives us:

$$(A \vee B) \rightarrow (C \rightarrow (D \;\&\; E))$$
$$(A \vee B)$$
$$\therefore (C \rightarrow (D \;\&\; E))$$

Thus we know that this is a valid argument because it is an instance of a valid argument-form. All valid arguments are either substitution instances of basic valid argument-forms, or are made up of steps that are such substitution instances.

5.27 Finally, in propositional logic the system is made more powerful as a way of establishing the validity of arguments by the addition of rules of *logical equivalence*. That is, the expressions are truth-functionally identical, in which case one expression can always be replaced by the other. Any logical expression can be replaced in a formula by any other expression that it is logically equivalent to.

10 *De Morgan's Theorems* (De. M)

$$\sim(p \;\&\; q) \equiv (\sim p \vee \sim q)$$

$$\sim(p \vee q) \equiv (\sim p \;\&\; \sim q)$$

11 *Commutation* (Com)

$$(p \vee q) \equiv (q \vee p)$$

$$(p \;\&\; q) \equiv (q \;\&\; p)$$

12 *Association* (Assoc)

$$(p \vee (q \vee r)) \equiv ((p \vee q) \vee r)$$

$$(p \;\&\; (q \;\&\; r)) \equiv ((p \;\&\; q) \;\&\; r)$$

13 *Distribution* (Dist)

$$(p \mathbin{\&} (q \vee r)) \equiv ((p \mathbin{\&} q) \vee (p \mathbin{\&} r))$$

$$(p \vee (q \mathbin{\&} r)) \equiv ((p \vee q) \mathbin{\&} (p \vee r))$$

14 *Double Negation* (DN)

$$p \equiv {\sim}{\sim}p$$

15 *Transposition* (Trans)

$$(p \rightarrow q) \equiv ({\sim}q \rightarrow {\sim}p)$$

16 *Material Implication* (Impl)

$$(p \rightarrow q) \equiv ({\sim}p \vee q)$$

17 *Material Equivalence* (Equiv)

$$(p \equiv q) \equiv ((p \rightarrow q) \mathbin{\&} (q \rightarrow p))$$

$$(p \equiv q) \equiv ((p \mathbin{\&} q) \vee ({\sim}p \mathbin{\&} {\sim}q))$$

18 *Exportation* (Exp)

$$((p \mathbin{\&} q) \rightarrow r) \equiv (p \rightarrow (q \rightarrow r))$$

19 *Tautology* (Taut)

$$p \equiv (p \vee p)$$

$$p \equiv (p \mathbin{\&} p)$$

5.28 *Deduction in propositional logic using rules of inference.* This is a more complex example of a valid argument in symbols using the rules of inference, including the rules of logical equivalence. The argument is valid overall because each step is either a premise or a step that is valid according to one of the nine deductive rules just listed. If each step is a valid step, then the move from the first step to the last step must be valid. The obverse is of course the case: if an argument is invalid, then the move from the first step to the last step must include at least one invalid step.

Below, lines 1–5 and before the ∴ are the premises. What follows the ∴ is the conclusion of the argument. The right-hand column under the conclusion gives the numbers that refer to the line or lines that the rule given after those numbers is applied to.

1.	A	
2.	$A \rightarrow \sim \sim B$	
3.	$B \rightarrow C$	
4.	$A \rightarrow D$	
5.	$C \ \& \ D$	∴E
6.	$\sim \sim B$	1,2, MP
7.	B	6, DN
8.	C	3,7, MP
9.	D	1,4, MP
10.	$C \ \& \ D$	8,9, Conj
11.	E	5,10, MP

Step 11 is the conclusion that is shown to follow deductively from the premises 1–5. Thus we have shown the argument to be valid. One could show the same thing by constructing a truth-table for the entire argument, but because there are 5 different letters used the truth-table would have 32 lines (2^n lines, when n is the number of different letters involved; in this case 5: A, B, C, D, E) giving all the possible combinations of assigning true and false values.

5.29 Predicate logic. This is an extension of propositional logic, and is in fact inclusive of it. No change in the basic idea of deductive logic and what constitutes a valid argument is involved. The main advance is that it enables us to deal in symbolic form with arguments that could not be properly represented in propositional logic: arguments that are not mere compounds of propositions. This is because predicate logic allows us to symbolise argument-forms in a way that looks within whole propositions; it allows us to symbolise argument-forms that involve the constituents of proposition and not just whole propositions.

Take the example of the following argument.

All Scotsmen have red hair
Some philosophers are Scotsmen
_____

Some philosophers have red hair

Let:

> A = All Scotsmen have red hair
> B = Some philosophers are Scotsmen
> C = Some philosophers have red hair

Then the argument according to propositional logic looks like this:

> A
> B
> _____
> $\therefore C$

Using this notation of propositional logic alone it *appears* invalid. Although we know that if an argument is a substitution-instance of a valid argument-form it is a valid argument, this example just goes to show that not all arguments that are substitution-instances of an invalid argument-form are thereby invalid, for they may also be substitution-instances of some valid argument-form. So in fact in this case the argument is valid, but the symbolic resources of propositional logic are not sufficient to make this apparent. The validity of the argument depends not on the truth-value of a complex (or compound) of whole simple propositions, but on the inner structure of the propositions. What is needed is the machinery of predicate logic.

5.30 The predicate logic carries with it all the machinery of the propositional logic. The crucial additional features in predicate logic are fourfold.

1   The use of the letters a, b, c . . . as constants that stand in place of individual names.
2   The use of the letters F, G, H . . . to stand in place of predicates that ascribe properties to things.
3   The use of the letters x, y, z . . . as variables that can stand for unspecified things.
4   The use of the quantifiers. The universal quantifier $\forall$ means 'all' (that is, 'every') and the existential quantifier $\exists$ means 'some' (that is, 'at least one'). So the expression $(\forall x)$ means:

'for all x . . . ', ('every x') and the existential quantifier $(\exists x)$ means 'for some x . . . ' ('at least one x').

Example
$(\forall x)(Mx)$ would, where 'M' stands for the predicate 'moves', symbolise the sentence, 'All things move' (that is, 'Everything moves'). One might write this as: 'For all x, x moves.'

Example
$(\exists x)(Mx)$ would, where 'M' stands for the predicate 'moves', symbolise the sentence, 'Some thing moves' (that is, 'At least one thing moves'). One might write this as: 'For some x, x moves.'

The quantifiers are used to 'bind' the variables over which they range. That is, they apply to variables and say how many (all, some, none) of the things we are talking about have the property ascribed to them by the predicate.

5.31 Four of the commonest forms are these.

$(\forall x)(Fx \rightarrow Gx)$	All things with F have G
$(\forall x)(Fx \rightarrow {\sim}Gx)$	No things with F have G
$(\exists x)(Fx \ \& \ Gx)$	Some things have F and have G
$(\exists x)(Fx \ \& \ {\sim}Gx)$	Some things have F and do not have G

5.32 We can now deal with the argument we were having trouble symbolising, in such a way that we do justice to the fact that it is plainly valid.

All Scotsmen have red hair
Some philosophers are Scotsmen
_____

Some philosophers have red hair

Let:

$Fx = x$ is a philosopher
$Gx = x$ is a Scotsman
$Hx = x$ has red hair

We can now symbolise the argument as follows.

$$(\forall x)(Gx \rightarrow Hx)$$
$$(\exists x)(Fx \ \& \ Gx)$$

———————————

$$(\exists x)(Fx \ \& \ Hx)$$

It reads as:

For all x, if x is a Scotsman then x has red hair
For some x, x is a philosopher and is a Scotsman

———————————

For some x, x is a philosopher and has red hair

This argument is valid.

5.33 *Quantification rules.* To establish the validity of an argument is to show that the conclusion follows from the premises. We may need to treat of propositions as less than whole and look inside them. For that we need in addition to the rules of inference of the propositional logic, four more *quantification rules*, telling us how the quantifiers can be properly used within deductions. Deductions are conducted in just the same way when they involve predication as when they involved only propositions. Each step, if the overall argument is to be valid, has to be a valid step; if the overall argument is invalid it must be because one of the steps is invalid.

The quantification rules are rather complex, and their application would extend this book beyond its intended purpose – to introduce to readers the natures of good arguments so that they may study more critically – and so I shall not state them here. I refer the reader to the many excellent logic texts listed in the Further Reading.

5.34 *Assessing arguments using natural deduction.* As with the rules of inference method, this method arises because truth-tables become hard to use with long complex arguments. But the result of each method is essentially the same. Both methods have advantages and disadvantages compared with the other.

Most of the machinery of the natural deductive system we have already covered in introducing the symbolic logic generally. It is possible therefore to go straight on to considering the method itself.

The outline of the natural deductive system is really very easy to articulate. We have already seen that the arguments we deal with are made up of strings of propositions linked by operators of both the propositional logic and the predicate logic. The natural deductive method simply gives rules as to when it is valid to *introduce* and *eliminate* the operators in arguments.

5.35 One example will suffice for the reader to get the hang of this, and intuitively see the legitimacy of the method. Take the operator &: a rule can be given for its legitimate introduction into an argument and for its legitimate elimination in an argument. Here is the introduction rule (I&) for &. Given that one has *A* and one has *B* we may derive (*A* & *B*). The intuitive sense of this is that if one has *A* and one has *B*, it makes sense to say that one therefore has both in the form of (*A* & *B*).

The treatment of all the other operators, including the quantifiers, is the same: there is a rule for the operator's introduction and for its elimination in an argument. Provided these rules are always followed – that is, each step is an instance of applying either the introduction or elimination rule – then the argument is valid, otherwise it is invalid.

5.36 *Natural deduction rules.*

1 *assumption*
   Any proposition may be introduced at any point in the argument
2 ∼ *elimination*
   Given a contradiction (*A* & ∼*A*), derive *B*
3 ∼ ∼ *introduction*
   Given *A*, derive ∼ ∼*A*
4 ∼ ∼ *elimination*
   Given ∼ ∼*A*, derive *A*
5 → *introduction*
   Given the conditional derivation from *A* of *B*, derive *A* → *B*
6 → *elimination*
   Given *A* and *A* → *B*, derive *B*

7 **& *introduction***
   Given A and B, derive $A \& B$

8 **& *elimination***
   Given $A \& B$, derive either A or derive B

9 **v *introduction***
   Given either A or given B, derive $A \vee B$

10 **v *elimination***
   Given $A \vee B$ and a derivation of C assuming A and also a derivation of C assuming B, derive C

11 **≡ *introduction***
   Given the derivation from A of B and the derivation from B of A, derive $A \equiv B$

12 **≡ *elimination***
   Given A and $A \equiv B$, or given A and $B \equiv A$, derive B

5.37 *Deduction in propositional logic using natural deduction rules.* It will be noted that this is the same deduction as already done above, using the rules of inference method. The result is the same.

1	A	
2	$A \to {\sim}{\sim}B$	
3	$B \to C$	
4	$A \to D$	
5	$C \& D$	$\therefore$ E
6	${\sim}{\sim}B$	1,2, $\to$ elim
7	B	6, ${\sim}{\sim}$ elim
8	C	3,7, $\to$ elim
9	D	1,4, $\to$ elim
10	$C \& D$	8,9, & intro
11	E	5,10, $\to$ elim

5.38 As has been said, the system adhered to here is called classical logic. It should now be revealed that the system of classical logic is not the only possible system of logic. However, classical logic is the most common logical system, and there is usually considerable overlap between the valid theorems of any alternative system and those of classical logic. The reader will have to attend to the Further Reading at the end of the book in order to explore the range of systems. The idea of alternative logics is an interesting and exciting one; it raises deep logical and philosophical questions, but they are beyond what can be covered in this book.

6

UNDERSTANDING REASON
IS NOT ENOUGH

6.1 Telling people what the nature of reason is is only effective and perhaps worthwhile if they can be induced to reason in the first place. There are all sorts of causes or forces that might make them not do so. This is just a fact about human beings, and is what is meant by saying that understanding reason is not enough. It is not the fault of the nature of reason itself that we fail to use it or use it properly. The *act of reasoning*, as opposed to *reason itself*, is something we *do*, and as such it is open to the influence of causal processes because the act of reasoning is itself a causal process. Neither the nature of reason itself – because it is not a causal process at all – nor the understanding of reason – because its influence is not powerful enough – is enough to ensure that people use reason and use it well. Reason cannot force us to reason. Understanding reason is not enough. The threat to arguing well, or good reasoning, stems often from features of our psychology other than an inability to grasp rational principles. The aim here is to indicate what lessons can be learned from the fact that psychological factors undermine our ability to argue well, and what can be done to oppose such factors. We are not purely logical creatures. We have a faculty of reason, an ability and sometimes a causal inclination to reason, but this is not enough to control those powerful non-rational processes that lead us to fail to reason, but nevertheless cause us to have beliefs, when reasoning is what we should have been doing. A way will be described whereby we can be surer that we implement reasoned argument. To get the benefit out of reasoning we need to start reasoning.

By analogy, it is no use merely *knowing* what you have to do in order to maintain your house roof or your car. For this knowledge to have any effect on the potential deterioration of either, one must apply that knowledge and overcome all those obstacles that cause one not to apply it.

6.2 Does being a skilled logician and precise reasoner in some field guarantee that you will apply reason when you should and not succumb to prejudice and illusion? No. Logicians and precise reasoners in particular fields are just as susceptible to the causes that blind them in certain cases, to such an extent that they hold beliefs without examining them rationally when they should. Isaac Newton practised alchemy. Nazi Germany and Communist Russia had many brilliant academics and scientists capable of precise reasoning who supported regimes whose theoretical bases were faulty, and whose practices were disastrous and produced terrible harm and oppression.

6.3 A few distinctions need to be made before proceeding.

• A rational process is one that obeys the laws of logic.

   Example

   All men are mortal, Socrates is a man, therefore Socrates is mortal.

• An irrational process is one that breaks the laws of logic.

   Example

   All men are mortal, Socrates is a man, therefore Socrates is tall.

• A non-rational process is one that cannot be said either to obey or to break the laws of logic; such processes simply *happen*.

   Example

   A tree falling on me.

6.4 We have to be clear at the outset what is *not* being asserted. What is not being asserted is that we ought to revert to some sort of *irrationality* when seeking true beliefs, that we ought to give up on good arguments in our attempt to have true beliefs. Of course irrational processes *may* lead us to true propositions; but if they do so they do so only by chance, a sort of luck. This is because there is no real logical connection between the conclusions and the propositions on which they are supposedly based; that is, the conclusion could be supposed false while the premises could be supposed true; although the conclusion could happen, even in this case, to be true – the point is that the conclusion does not follow from the premises.

6.5 Non-rational processes may lead us to argue badly or not at all, when we should be reasoning and reasoning well. The way in which non-rational processes do this fits exactly with the way in which arguments can fail. The *bad* non-rational processes lead us to disregard one or both of the ways in which arguments can fail, or make mistakes in judging these ways, in situations where considering the quality of the argument is exactly what we should be doing. First, the bad non-rational processes lead us either to fail to consider whether there are premises being given at all for the conclusion we are expected to accept or, if they are considered, to come to accept false premises as true. Second, the bad non-rational processes lead us to disregard validity or to accept invalid steps in arguments. Again, we may still hit upon the truth in the conclusion. But it is a dangerous game; we have only hit upon the truth by luck. We were lucky this time perhaps, but the next time we may not be. We should therefore try to apply reason in such cases.

6.6 Let us look at a true story that illustrates some of the points being made. In the 1930s a Jewish socialist journalist attended a Nazi rally held at Nuremberg. He was hardly a person favourably inclined to what he was witnessing. Hitler was on the platform addressing a huge crowd and demonstrating his skill in mass oratory before an enthusiastic audience. Much of what Hitler had to say was in the form of unsubstantiated assertions presented without argument and delivered in heated emotive language. No doubt much of it was anti-Semitic and deeply hostile to the socialism the reporter believed in. Nevertheless, after about half an hour of the tirade from Hitler, the Jewish socialist journalist started to feel left out; he felt the pull to belong, he wanted to feel a part of this body of people and to share in the beliefs of the enthusiastic Nazi supporters. Was this because he was suddenly convinced by arguments he was hearing as to the truth of the beliefs being asserted? This is hardly likely. Not only was there hardly any argument presented for these beliefs, but what there was consisted of poor argument that failed to support the beliefs. The explanation is one of psychology, not of logic. The atmosphere in which the reporter heard the speech was one of warm jubilation arranged to engender a feeling of collective strength, well-being and togetherness. It seems to be a feature of human nature that often there is a strong tendency to want to be a part of such collective activities even in disregard of their merits. An element of being a part of such a gathering involves sharing beliefs. It is just a fact about human beings that in the right circumstances they find it hard to resist coming to hold the beliefs of those around them, no matter how absurd or unsubstantiated those beliefs may be in many cases. So what led to the unlikely situation of a Jewish socialist reporter desiring, albeit in passing, oneness of belief with those who clearly should have been anathema to him, was some sort of psychological fact about human beings combined with the facts of a certain situation. Nothing to do with reasoning at all. If it could have such power over this reporter, little wonder that those already sympathetic to what was being said found it all but overwhelming, and easy to be firmly convinced of the truth of the claims that were being asserted, regardless of the quality or indeed the existence of arguments.

6.7 There are various explanations for why people come to hold that certain propositions are true. One possible explanation might certainly be that they have followed the course of a good argument and ended up with a belief that is true because of this. There are, however, many other routes to holding beliefs that may or may not actually be true, and may or may not have a good argument for their truth.

6.8 Here we must remind ourselves that good argument may as a matter of psychological fact end up convincing no one: the conclusion really does follow from the premises, but it does not result in people actually believing the conclusion. One reason might be that the argument, although valid, is too complex to follow; another might be that people are not open to reason. We must also remember that there are many non-rational processes, such as persuasion through propaganda and peer pressure, that end up with people holding beliefs even though they have not in fact been presented with any good arguments for those beliefs. Not all of these processes are bad in themselves. If I tell my young daughter not to play with fire, that in itself, although not an argument, is a good enough reason for her to believe she should not play with fire. Until she can understand properly it would be absurd for me to give her an argument. But it must be noted that my mere instruction is only a reason for her not to play with fire because there *is* a good argument why she should not.

What the multitude of non-rational routes that result in beliefs are is a subject for empirical psychology. Moreover, tracing what people actually do, even supposing it to be universally the case, has nothing to do with the logic of good reasoning. Logic is not concerned with what people *do* but what they *ought to do* if they want to reason well. It is in this sense that logic is said to be *prescriptive* or *normative*, not factual.

6.9 Logic is prescriptive or normative, not factual; it gives an account of good reasoning; it cannot itself *force* us to reason in the first place or, when we attempt to reason, guarantee we will reason well in accordance with the principles of good logic. It can tell us what we ought to do if we want to reason at all and well. It cannot impel us to begin to reason, or to stick to it. For that more is required, something not only outside logic, but also something in addition to the natural inclination to reason that comes from our faculty of reason.

6.10 An understanding of logic and its rules, our faculty of reason, *may* cause us to reason and reason well when we should – it may have some psychological power to do this – but other causal forces are at work both without and within our minds. This does not contradict the claim that *logic itself* is properly characterised totally independently of psychology and causes; it is not logic that has causal effects or can be affected causally, but the psychological process of people *thinking* the rules of logic – the activity of our faculty of reason. Psychologically processes can consist of thinking that is in accord with the rules of logic, and we may even have a natural inclination to do such thinking. Such a psychological process is a causal process. Of course what *is* reason and good reasoning is in no way dependent on whether anyone reasons at all. However, often other causal forces are in play that induce us not to begin reasoning or to follow reason. We need to counter these causal forces by other *causal* forces – forces in addition to whatever tendency we may have to reason even when we understand how to do so – because we are not purely logical creatures. A machine might be devised that only ever proceeded by logical steps in accordance with the rules of deductive reasoning – it would have no need for strategies to counter its tendency to move in non-logical steps, to abandon reason – but we are not such a machine. We need such strategies in addition to knowing what is good reasoning.

6.11 What we need to do to reason well, in addition to knowing the rules of good reasoning (implicitly or explicitly), is to take steps to guard against the ways in which non-rational forces can result in our failing to reason at all or our failing to reason competently. This applies in those situations where reasoning is what we should be doing. We need to be alert, aware, and on our guard, to the ways in which our reasoning can be undermined by forces that are inclined to sweep us along when we should in fact step back and reason about a particular matter.

6.12 This can be a long-term or short-term problem. Longstanding habits of thought may prevent us from considering a problem rationally. Short-term powerful forces can propel us to a belief before we know it.

It is one thing to know the theory of good reasoning; it is another matter to put that theory into practice. In the extreme case, as we have said, there is nothing contradictory about an outstanding logician who holds strange and implausible beliefs. He may start from false premises; he may disregard validity; he may simply not begin to reason at all.

Of course one might hope that knowing about good reasoning, the faculty of reason, would have some psychological effect on people, and tend to result in them thinking more rationally. But knowing is frequently not sufficient.

History bears this out: what has in the past convinced people has often had little or nothing to do with the quality of the argument with which they were presented. Otherwise sophisticated people managed to convince themselves that Jews were non-human; that human nature is infinitely pliable to its core and so can be disregarded and crushed; that some women are witches, that some people can cast evil spells over others; that the stars can determine or predict our lives; huge groups have believed that disease, deformity and handicap is a punishment for sin. Nothing fundamental in this respect has changed today; people are, and probably always will be, prone to techniques, methods, and influences involving little or no argument, that convince them to believe certain things, and then often to act on those beliefs. One of the major influences is often simply what everyone else thinks. Good reasoning is not synonymous with the power to convince. Good reasoning may have the power to convince, but we cannot be sure because it is not that power that defines what good reasoning is; in addition reasoning is not the only force that psychologically operates within us, and operates on us from without, that determines our beliefs. There are ways of convincing people other than by presenting them with good argument, ways which can substitute for and often run counter to the arguments, that mean that grasping reason is not enough to be sure that people will think rationally.

6.13 One might conclude from this that in order to be rational one must always go through the processes of seeing whether one is presented with true premises from which a conclusion follows. But this would be a mistake and absurd. If I am walking down the street under some trees in normal circumstances (not, say, in a hurricane) it would be ridiculous to construct an argument on the likelihood of the trees falling on me. What is required for a rational life is that reason, in the sense of constructing or considering an argument, is applied *appropriately*. In cases such as our walking under trees in normal circumstances, it is indeed *rational* not to subject our beliefs on a daily basis to logical examination. We have large stacks of beliefs that we have acquired about the world, and use instinctively, which it would be absurd to go around continually questioning and subjecting to logical analysis. In fact there are good arguments as to why it would be absurd and not rational to apply arguments all the time to our beliefs.

6.14 Another misconception is that living rationally involves negating and suppressing our emotions all the time. This too is false. Emotions, it is true, are one of the major causes of our failing to think rationally when we should and of our making errors in our reasoning when we do think rationally. But it would be quite inappropriate for me to apply rational analysis to whether I liked a particular piece of music or not. Interestingly, it would be appropriate to apply arguments to the question of whether the music was any good or not. But that is a different question. The issue is not one of subsuming emotion in an attempt to live life by only the icy consideration of logic – to become a creature ruled by pure logic. Emotion might even motivate us to consider arguments in the first place and examine them with care when we should do so. The issue is one of when emotion is appropriate in our lives, and when we may need to set emotion aside and consider the arguments. Before anyone defends emotion too vehemently and sees reasoning as a threat to his right to have powerful and personal emotional reactions (many of which are perfectly reasonable), he should consider the surgeon who might be about to operate on him, and wonder at the degree to which he would like the surgeon to be motivated by emotion in his beliefs about the course of treatment.

6.15 *Habits*. One thing that may induce us to reason when we should and to reason well is seeing clearly the dangers of not doing so; this itself may motivate us to reason. However, I believe just pointing this out and seeing this is not enough to ensure that we reason appropriately. We need something more to strengthen the tendency to reason appropriately.

Arguments as such operate against arguments (one argument may refute another) and non-rational forces operate against non-rational forces (one set of processes may happen to alter or be prevented by another). The act of reasoning consists of thoughts that are causal processes and are therefore subject to causal – non-rational – effects. This is true even though the thoughts may be in accord with the dictates of thinking rationally as described by the principles of good reasoning. From this it follows that we can be caused not to reason at all, or, if we start, to reason badly. Too frequently this is true.

Habits are one of the most powerful non-rational forces within us; habits can be a force for the good that can be trained. What we need are *good habits* which cause us to reason when we should to counter bad forces (sometimes themselves also habits) that cause us not to reason well or not to reason at all when we should. Many of the non-rational forces that would prevent us from reasoning when we should are so powerful that the only way to counter them is to set up countervailing non-rational forces that usher in the use of reason. Note how the arachnophobe may rationally know that the spider is not dangerous (he may accept the soundness of the argument leading to that conclusion), but may nevertheless be unable to apply reason to his fearful beliefs about spiders in such a way as to make any difference to those beliefs. Thus there is the need to build up strong countervailing forces in the form of good habits that themselves *cause* us to reason when we should – a habitual tendency that is a force for good ingrained within us.

6.16 *Rational habits.* We can build up the good habits that lead us to apply reason when we should by practising reasoning and applying it to our beliefs, especially in circumstances where forces operate to make it hard for us to start reasoning or, if we start, to reason well. In this way the muscle of reason will be built up. Next time we need it, and should apply it, it will be both inclined to come into action and in good shape for what it needs to do. Moreover, this strategy works best when it becomes a feature of our lives; when it is a long-term stance which cultivates a well-ingrained habit; when it becomes a way of life in a multitude of small and large ways.

6.17 Let me sum up my thoughts on these matters so far as follows. What is important is that we always both leave the door ajar for the rational consideration of all our beliefs, and learn to find mechanisms whereby we examine our beliefs rationally when appropriate; we must guard against the non-rational processes that lead us to accept things as true when we should be using reason, and we must build up habits that do so through practising all our lives on subjects that we find difficult to address. The acquiring of these habits is the best way to counter the forces ranged against our reasoning when reasoning is what we should be doing.

6.18 *Three lessons about reasoning.* We have three issues and three answers.

(a) What constitutes the failure of a logical argument when an argument is presented?

No good reason has been presented for the conclusion being true.

One ought to accept a conclusion in an argument as true only if the argument is a good one. Determining whether the argument is a good one means deciding whether the proposition standing as the conclusion follows from other true propositions standing as the premises.

(b) What are the appropriate circumstances under which logical argument should be applied?

We should beware of those situations, and apply reason, where we know or think it likely, both that powerful non-rational forces may be operating to undermine reasoning and that reason, rather than anything else, is the best way of acquiring the truth.

Sometimes they may be circumstances in which the matters are important and circumstances abnormal. These two features taken together should alert us to the fact that we have some thinking to do, and in many instances either condition being satisfied may be sufficient. It is, however, impossible to rule out various other situations in which reasoning is desirable. Such a case might be where there are important matters at stake, and where we think that the belief in the truth of certain propositions has become suspicious because it is going unquestioned.

(c) What steps can we take to make it more likely that we apply logical argument when we should?

We should find ways to acquire good mental habits that cause us to reason against whatever bad forces we may encounter, that tend to prevent reason being applied properly or at all when it should be, by practising reasoning in situations where we find it difficult psychologically to do so, and we should make such a way of thinking a feature of our lives.

One should learn ways to adopt good mental habits that counteract circumstances in which one is tempted not to apply reason when one should. We can best build up this habit over our life by practising applying reason to things we regard as true, cases where we find it hard to apply reason, cases perhaps where we feel uncomfortable or disturbed in engaging in rational examination. In this way we will build up the capacity to apply reason automatically as a habit of our life when we should, and counter those forces that work to prevent this; the force of rational habit will make it more likely that we will reason when we should.

6.19 Part of the problem here is that it is a bit like trying to lift oneself up by one's own bootlaces. Those circumstances in which one fails to apply reason when one should are often precisely those circumstances in which it is difficult to remember to, or make oneself, apply reason; if one had remembered and could have, then one would have done so. But the problem of lifting oneself up by one's own bootlaces is overcome by generally adopting and harnessing the force of good mental habits in order to reason.

An analogy here might be the way that the army gets soldiers to assemble and disassemble guns in the dark or blindfolded. The idea is not so much that this is what they will often have to do, as that if they can do it with their eyes shut then doing it with their eyes open will be easy. In the same way runners often train with weights on their backs; when they come to do it without the weights they are much stronger than they would have been otherwise and the running is easier.

6.20 *Practice.* There are rational equivalents of these skills and physical activities. To start with it is a matter of always leaving the door ajar on one's beliefs; having at the back of one's mind that one might be mistaken and that reason should be applied, especially in circumstances well known to induce one to believe certain things regardless, or indeed in disregard, of reason. It is the ability to keep this openness at the back of one's mind and bring it to the fore even when forces are running against it that constitutes the good habits needed to apply reason when one should.

How one gets into this state is by *practice*, that is, by doing it in the first place and then continuing until it becomes an instinctive and ingrained reaction; it becomes a habit in fact. When the issue is whether something is true or false – and reason in that case is the way to discover the truth – one must, in circumstances where there are powerful forces leading one to ignore reason altogether, start to apply reason. After a while the application of reason will itself become habitual and immediate even in these circumstances. Of course one has to take the first step. Little can really help in this, except to point out the dangers of not reasoning, the advantages of reasoning, and that there are in fact powerful forces operating which cause us to fail to adopt a rational stance at all, when reason is what we should be applying in our concern for the truth.

6.21 *The morality of reason.* Part of the point being made here concerns the morality of reason and of adopting mental habits that cause us to apply reason when we should. There are many circumstances in which we should not only apply reason if we want to find out the truth, but in which it is also important that it is the truth that we set our minds on. In fact there are two senses of 'should' in play here: we should apply reason to discover the truth, and we should apply reason because a failure to discover the truth matters and might be unethical, perhaps leading to terrible consequences.

For example, suppose I want to find out the distance of the tenth nearest star. I think it is obvious that we *should* think in a rational way in order to find out the answer. But suppose I do not bother; perhaps nothing very serious or harmful will follow. Now take another example: suppose I am trying to decide if Stalin is so evil that I ought to try to kill him. In this case it is important not only that I should reason in order to find out the truth, but also that I should, in a moral sense, apply reason because having a false belief could have terrible and harmful consequences. Thus reason matters; it matters because the truth matters; and the truth matters because false beliefs can have terrible and harmful consequences. In addition, not seeking the truth belittles us as human beings and diminishes our freedom. This is why learning to reason well, and finding ways to induce oneself to apply reason when one should, even when forces operate against one's doing so, is not a trivial game. It matters that one knows how to reason well and that one actually does so when one should. It matters because false beliefs can lead to harmful consequences – and often do so, because our beliefs are important determinants of our actions. This is true for beliefs concerning both facts and values.

6.22 *Summary.* Reason and applying reason matters because it is a major way of finding the truth, and finding the truth about important matters. Circumstances and forces, in addition to a lack of understanding of reason, operate to undermine reasoning. We can find out how to reason well and how to examine the reasoning of others. We can counter the forces that would undermine reasoning, and lead us to fail to reason well or at all, by practising reasoning about matters where these very forces operate most strongly and where we therefore find it hard to reason. In this way, when we encounter situations where strong forces operate and tend to disarm reason where we should be reasoning, we will be ready for them, and by force of habit will not succumb to the neglect of reason. This book both sets out the principles of good reasoning (using only true premises and valid arguments) so they are understood, and urges a route to applying them (rational habits derived from practice) more surely when they should be applied, even in the face of forces that can cause them to be applied poorly or not at all. The route urged here is to think of what it is that you find hard to question and reason about; try to reason about it; see whether the belief is really based on decent evidence. That way you will not only rationally examine those matters, and become better at reasoning, but you will also come to reason when you should.

FURTHER READING

The aim of this list is to give the reader access to a cross-section of further reading. The technical logic books listed go beyond the basic level of this book. Some of the books that cover the application of logic to everyday reasoning I have some disagreement with; but it is important and, indeed, consistent with the aspirations of this book, that the reader be made aware of various approaches. My other reason for including the following books is of course to give credit to many of the works I have learnt from over the years. I have marked with an asterisk * the books I think would make a good next step for those wanting to pursue the more formal aspects of logic.

Boylan, Michael *The Process of Argument* (Lanham: University Press of America, 1993).

Carey, Stephen *The Uses and Abuses of Argument* (Mountain View, California: Mayfield Publishing Company, 2000).

Cohen, Morris R. & Nagel, Ernest *An Introduction to Logic and Scientific Method* (Routledge, 1961).

Conway, David A. & Munson, Ronald *Elements of Reasoning* (Belmont, California: Wadsworth Press, 1990).

Copi, Irving & Cohen, Carl *Introduction to Logic* (New York: Prentice Hall, 1997, 10th edition).*

Ellis, Brian *Rational Belief Systems* (Oxford: Blackwell, 1979).

Emmet, E. R. *The Use of Reason* (London: Longman, 1960).

Fisher, Alec *The Logic of Real Arguments* (Cambridge: Cambridge University Press, 1988).

Fitch, Frederic B. *Symbolic Logic* (New York: Ronald Press, 1952).*

Flew, Anthony *Thinking About Thinking* (London: Fontana, 1990).

Forbes, Graham *Modern Logic: A Text Book in Elementary Symbolic Logic* (Oxford: Oxford University Press, 1994).

Geach, Peter *Reason and Argument* (Oxford: Basil Blackwell, 1976).

Guttenplan, Samuel *The Language of Logic* (Oxford: Basil Blackwell, 1986).

Haack, Susan *Philosophy of Logics* (Cambridge: Cambridge University Press, 1978).

Harman, Gilbert *Change in View: Principles of Reasoning* (Cambridge Mass: MIT Press, 1989).

Hintikka, Jaakko & Bachman, James *What if–: Towards Excellence in Reasoning* (San Francisco: Mayfield Publishing Company, 1991).*

Hodgers, Wilfred *Logic* (London: Penguin, 1991).

Hurley, Patrick J. *A Concise Introduction to Logic* (Belmont, California: Wadsworth, 1997).

Iseminger, Gary (ed.) *Logic and Philosophy* (New York: Appleton-Century-Croft, 1968).

Kahane, Howard *Logic and Philosophy* (Belmont, California: Wadsworth, 1990, 6th edition).*

—— *Logic and Contemporary Rhetoric: The Use of Reason in Everyday Life* (Belmont, California: Wadsworth, 1992, 6th edition).

Kelly, David *The Art of Reasoning* (New York: W. W. Norton, 1988).

Kirwan, Christopher *Logic and Argument* (London: Duckworth, 1978).

Lemmon, E. J. *Beginning Logic* (London: Nelson, 1981).*

Mates, Benson *Elementary Logic* (Oxford: Oxford University Press, 1965).

Newton-Smith, W. H. *Logic* (London: Routledge, 1990).*

Prior, Arthur N. *Formal Logic* (Oxford: Oxford University Press, 1973).

Quine, W. V. *Elementary Logic* (Harvard: Harvard University Press, 1980, revised edition).*

—— *Methods of Logic* (Harvard: Harvard University Press, 1989, 4th edition).

Read, Stephen *Thinking About Logic* (Oxford: Oxford University Press, 1994).

Restall, Greg *Logic* (London: UCL Press, 2000).*

Robinson, Richard *Definition* (Oxford: Clarendon Press, 1950).

Sainsbury, Mark *Logical Forms: An Introduction to Philosophical Logic* (Oxford: Basil Blackwell, 1991).

Salmon, Wesley C. *Logic* (New York: Prentice Hall, 1984, 3rd edition).

Shand, John *Philosophy and Philosophers: An Introduction to Western Philosophy* (London: Penguin, 1994).

Shaw, Patrick *Logic and Its Limits* (London: Pan Books, 1997, 2nd edition).

Simpson, R. L. *Essentials of Symbolic Logic* (London: Routledge, 1988).*

Strawson, Peter F. *Introduction to Logical Theory* (London: Methuen, 1966).

Tennant, Neil *Natural Logic* (Edinburgh: Edinburgh University Press, 1979).

Terrell, D. B. *A Modern Introduction to Deductive Reasoning* (New York: Holt, Rinehart & Winston, 1967).

Thomason, Richmond H. *Symbolic Logic* (London: Collier Macmillan, 1970).

Thomson, Anne *Practice in Reasoning* (London: Routledge, 1996).

Thouless, R. H. & Thouless, C. R. *Straight and Crooked Thinking* (London: Hodder & Stoughton, 1990, 4th edition).

Tomassi, Paul *Logic* (London: Routledge, 1999).*

Toulmin, Stephen *The Uses of Argument* (Cambridge: Cambridge University Press, 1958).

Toulmin, Stephen, Rieke, Richard & Janik, Allan *Introduction to Reasoning* (London: Macmillan, 1979).

Walton, Douglas *Informal Logic* (Cambridge: Cambridge University Press, 1989).

—— *The Place of Emotion in Argument* (Pennsylvania: Pennsylvania University Press, 1992).

Warburton, Nigel *Thinking From A to Z* (London: Routledge, 1996).

Weston, Anthony *A Rulebook for Argument* (Indianapolis: Hackett, 1992, 2nd edition).

INDEX